Easing Into
EasyLanguage
The Hi-Res Edition (2nd in Series)

George Pruitt

CONTENTS

INTRODUCTION

This book is for those that have read the Foundation Edition or have some experience working with EasyLanguage and the various functions that help make a trading decision. This book's audience will be those programmers that want to take an idea that requires intraday market movement observations to make a trading decision and then program it accurately. Now that you have programmed daily bar systems, you may want to drill down and add some components that require additional market information. If this is you, then you have come to the right place.

Tutorials 14, 15 and 16 deal with a trading algorithm that uses daily bars to calculate entries and exists, but are overlaid on five or one minute bars so that accurate entries and exits are performed. The close price you see on a daily bar is actually a settlement price, a theoretical price based on a specific time and the market action during the settlement period. By not using daily bars, it is up to the user to derive his own settlement prices. In these tutorials, the settlement time for the crude futures, for example, is 1430 or 2:30 p.m. ET time, so code is developed to derive an "unofficial" settlement price by examining the closing bar at 1430 and using a formula to extrapolate a price close to the official settlement price. A framework is introduced to allow the user to use different inputs that include using different settlement times and formulas.

Tutorial 17 starts the *day-trading* portion of the book. Algorithms are shown that use daily and non-daily bars to calculate entries and intraday minute bars to carry out the execution. The strategy is carried over to Tutorial 18 where it is used as the foundation to build a framework for further strategy development. A framework is a base strategy that allows the user to modify parameters to easily uncover more efficient and productive algorithms without having to recreate the wheel.

Tutorial 19 continues with the day trade scheme, but utilizes volatility and *open range break out* to develop its own framework. This tutorial also introduces code to enable a percent trailing stop exit. These day trade algorithms could be enabled to be auto-traded.

Tutorial 20 introduces the concept of pyramiding at different price levels on a day trading basis. These levels are brought to you by the enigmatic Camarilla equations. Accurate long and short entry accounting is presented as well. EasyLanguage provides an **AvgEntryPrice** keyword to acquire the average price of multiple single direction entries and it is used to develop a pyramid based percent trailing stop.

Tutorial 21 demonstrates "*put two on, take a profit on one, and pull the final stop to breakeven*" approach to day trading. After taking a profit, the second position becomes a free trade. The devil in this scheme is getting stopped out with two positions (units) on. Best case scenario you take a profit on the first and the final position is closed out with a profit too. An acceptable scenario is you take profit on the first and the second is stopped out at a breakeven point.

Tutorial 22 demonstrates the use of a **Finite State Machine (FSM)** to completely develop and code a day trading scheme where the intraday movement guides the algorithm to take a trade. The process of moving from one state to another, where transitions are defined by specific events is portrayed by the life of a worm as it transforms into a beautiful butterfly.

Tutorial 23 includes several generic templates that were derived from the earlier tutorials. These templates could be used as foundations to build your own research upon.

Website Link for Supplemental Material:
https://wp.me/P30hs2-2xN

The password is located at the end of the first paragraph of Tutorial 22.

ABOUT WEBSITE

Here is the link to the supplemental material. This includes the ELD for TradeStation and MultiCharts and the links to the videos in one convenient place.

https://wp.me/P30hs2-2xN

Password: Located at the end of the first paragraph of Tutorial 22.

COMPUTER CODE AND FONTS IN PRINT VERSION

This book is full of EasyLanguage code that should be mono-spaced - one space for each character. However, this font in Kindle Create does not allow for the mathematical symbols " = , >=, or <=". I had to to use the *Amazon Ember* font to seperate the computer code from the rest of the text. So, instead of getting this:

```
1    switch (lilBug)
2    begin
3        case("worm"):
4            if h > lilBugPeak then
5            begin
6                lilBugPeak = high;
7                lilBugPeakTime = t;
8            end;
9            if l < lilBugValley then
10           begin
11               lilBugValley = low;
12               lilBugValleyTime = t;
13           end;
14           if lilBugPeak - lilBugValley > bugDropRisePer * ATRValue then
15           begin
16               if lilBugValleyTime > lilBugPeakTime then
17               begin
18                   lilBug = "bullBug";
19               end;
20           end;
21           if lilBugPeak - lilBugValley > bugDropRisePer * ATRValue then
22           begin
23               if lilBugValleyTime < lilBugPeakTime then
24                   lilBug = "bearBug";
25           end;
```

You get this:

```
switch (lilBug)
begin
    case("worm"):
        if h > lilBugPeak then
        begin
            lilBugPeak = high;
```

```
        lilBugPeakTime = t;
    end;
    if l < lilBugValley then
    begin
        lilBugValley = low;
        lilBugValleyTime = t;
    end;
    if lilBugPeak - lilBugValley > bugDropRisePer * ATRValue then
    begin
        if lilBugValleyTime > lilBugPeakTime then
        begin
            lilBug = "bullBug";
    end;
    end;
    if lilBugPeak - lilBugValley > bugDropRisePer * ATRValue then
    begin
        if lilBugValleyTime < lilBugPeakTime then
            lilBug = "bearBug";
    end;
```

For this reason I have included a text file with a monospaced font in the supplemental download from my website. I hope this doesn't cause too much inconvenience. I am a stickler when it comes to the format of computer code, because it is easier to read and understand if done right.

USING EASYLANGUAGE TO PROGRAM ON MINUTE INTERVALS?

"Programming is the art of telling another human being what one wants the computer to do." Donald Knuth

EASYLANGUAGE can be used to program almost any idea, back-test it and then potentially automate its trade directives. Not all strategies that can be historically evaluated can be automated. If a strategy generates a trade signal during market hours, then most likely it can be automated. Some of the strategies presented in this edition could be automated. However, that is not the main purpose of the included tutorials. The overall objective of Hi-Res is to teach the syntax and the techniques to properly and accurately develop and test algorithms that rely on minute bars. Even simple concepts that need to know the flow of the market on an intraday basis require another level of understanding and programming constructs. If you want to program a strategy that can buy and sell short on the same day, then you need to drill down to a higher resolution of data. Now if you can only buy or sell (not both) based on some form of filtering, then daily bars would be fine. If you want to incorporate a protective stop and a profit objective that can occur on the same day, then you will need to test on minute data.

If you are only entering or exiting on the open or close of a daily

1

bar, then daily bars are fine here too. You will better understand these criteria after going through the first tutorial in this book. Throughout the tutorials I will be using five or one minute bars for all of the development of Strategies and other Analysis Techniques. I will start at Tutorial Fourteen since there were thirteen in *The Foundation Edition*. Don't worry if you haven't read the first book in the series, as long as you are comfortable with the first tutorial in this book you should be fine. If you are not, then I would suggest reading *The Foundation Edition*.

Which Time Zone Are You In And Why Is This So Important

I also assume the reader knows how to create an intraday (five or one minute bar) chart. It is quite simple, just create a new chart and then **Format Symbol...**

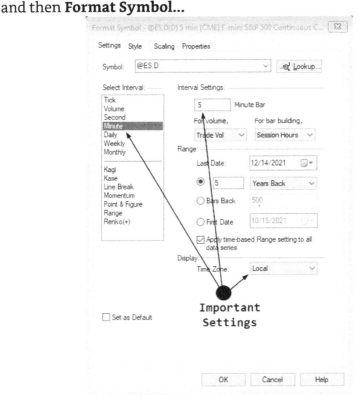

Here you select **Minute** as **Selected Interval** and then **5** for **Interval Settings**. I am using my **Local Time Zone** which is Eastern Time or ET. I discuss *the use of different times extensively and some of the Strategies that I present use Time as input*. If you are in a different time zone than ET, then you will need to adjust the time references and inputs accordingly. So, if I say 1700 or 5:00 p.m. as the end time of a trading session and you live in Los Angeles, then you will want to subtract 3 hours from my explanation or strategy inputs. Many of the markets and all stocks trade in my ET time zone so the Local and Exchange Times are the same. Let's take a look at a market (soybeans) that trades on an exchange located in the Central Time or CT zone (Chicago).

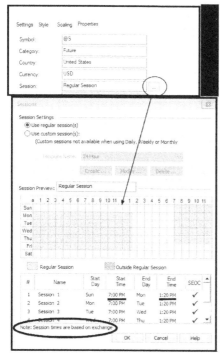

Here is a look at the Session Settings for a five minute bar chart of soybeans. Notice the session start and end times are described in the exchange's time zone. The soybean market opens the week on Sunday at 7:00 p.m. CT. In my ET time zone, this would be 8:00 p.m. The market closes the following day at 1:15 p.m. CT or 2:15 ET. In the Tutorials that follow, I might refer to the end session time as 2:15 p.m. or 1415 in military time. This time relates to my location in the ET. If you are in Chicago and use **Local** as your **Display Time Zone**, then you would need to mentally adjust my description to 1:15 p.m. or 1315. If you use **Local** and you reside in Los Angeles, then you would need to adjust my time reference of 2:15 p.m. to 11:15 a.m or 1115 military time. If I optimize a time input on this market from 11:15 a.m. to 2:15 p.m. and you live in LA, then you would optimize from 8:15 a.m. to 11:15 a.m. Notice the first bar of the trading session of this chart of soybeans.

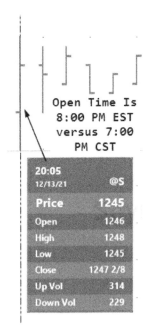

Open Time Is 8:00 PM EST versus 7:00 PM CST

20:05 12/13/21	@S
Price	1245
Open	1246
High	1248
Low	1245
Close	1247 2/8
Up Vol	314
Down Vol	229

It is 8:00 p.m. not 7:00 p.m. and this is because I display the data with ET time stamps (using the **LOCAL** setting). You can't imaging the confusion this can cause. In my life as a fund manager I was also a *System Assist* broker and traded customer derived algorithms for their own accounts, and whenever a time based user input was involved there was always a little bit of confusion. I traded a system from a California based client who used his local time in his time based inputs and variables. So when he originally sent the TradeStation workspace to me it reflected the **data** in **my local** time zone and his **time based variables** in **his local** time, which was three hours behind me. So right off the bat, my results did not match his. So we had to modify his time variables to reflect ET time. The best solution is to use **Exchange Time** for all chart displays. In doing so, there would be no need for time translation. However, most traders like to see *their* time zone on the time stamps on *their* own charts. Just keep this in my when going through the tutorials.

TUTORIAL 14 - WHY DO I NEED TO USE INTRADAY DATA

Many trading strategies (even simple ones) need to know what occurs first in an intraday market move. This first example strategy will sound exceedingly simple once I describe it, and it may seem to you it can be tested on a daily bar time frame.

Open Range Breakout With Profit Objective And Stop Loss

Long Entry: if close of yesterday is greater than the prior day's close, then buy 20% of yesterday's **true range** above the open tick, else buy 40% of yesterday's **true range** above the open tick. **Short Entry:** if close of yesterday is less than or equal to the prior day's close, then sell short 20% of yesterday's **true range** below the open tick, else sell short 40% of yesterday's **true range** below the open tick.

Long/Short Exit: take a $1000 profit or a $500 loss.

Sounds simple enough, right? Let's program it using a daily bar scheme and on daily bars. Here is the results of the programming going back five years - remember no execution costs.

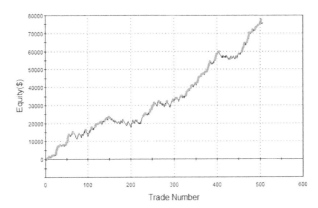

Sign me up right now! Looks too good to be true (**2G2BT**) and it is. Here is the code. Tell me where we went wrong.

```
//EZ_ORBO_DAILY BARS
if close > close[1] then
begin
    buy("Orbo20Buy") next bar at
        open of tomorrow + 0.20 * trueRange[1] stop;
    sellShort("Orbo40Shrt") next bar at
        open of tomorrow - 0.40 * trueRange[1] stop;
end
else
begin
    buy("Orbo40Buy") next bar at
        open of tomorrow + 0.40 * trueRange[1] stop;
    sellShort("Orbo20Shrt") next bar at
            open of tomorrow - 0.20 * trueRange[1] stop;
end;
setStopLoss(500);setProfitTarget(1000);
```

If you went through the Foundation edition, or have some EasyLanguage experience, everything will look just fine (notice the highlighted "**end**" and the lack of a semicolon - just a re-minder to leave the semicolon off when the next line is "else" or you will get an error message - **"This word cannot start a state-ment"**). The coding is perfect and the computer is doing exactly what it is being told. The idea of using different long and short entry levels based off the prior day's action can be attributed to George Douglas Taylor ("The Taylor Trading Method"). So what's the problem? Take a look a these few bars and see if you see any-thing suspicious.

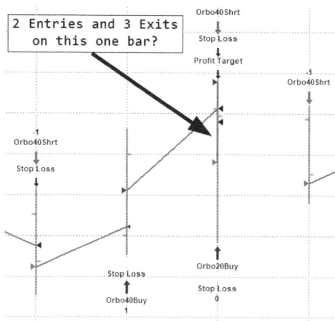

From left to right: bought near the high of the first bar and then stopped out on the next bar's open. Shorted near the low of the second bar and stopped out on the open of the following bar. Bought just past the midpoint on the third bar and then all he** breaks out on the fourth bar. I will let the computer explain what happened.

Strategy	
	Sell 1 @ 69.06
	Buy 1 @ 69.39
	Sell 1 @ 68.89
	Short 1 @ 68.40
	Cover 1 @ 68.90

So the long position that was initiated on the prior bar took a profit at 69.06 and since the market continued up, another buy was generated at 69.39. Sounds about right. It looks like that long position from 69.39 was liquidated at 68.89 with a $500 loss. The market continues down and a short order is triggered at 68.40 and then that position was covered at 68.90 for another $500 loss.

This could have really happened. Look at the bar formation once again.

Just looking at the expanded view it seems like the market opened and then went up and then collapsed and then rallied

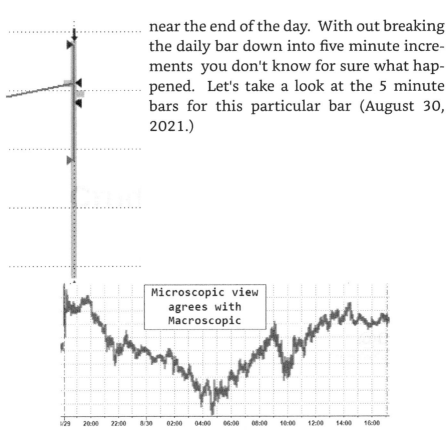

near the end of the day. With out breaking the daily bar down into five minute increments you don't know for sure what happened. Let's take a look at the 5 minute bars for this particular bar (August 30, 2021.)

Microscopic view agrees with Macroscopic

The market did exactly what we thought; opened up, rallied a hair, collapsed and rallied through to the rest of the day. Here is the same approach with 5 minute bars.

1:Take Profit
2:Go Long >>>
3:Exit Long
4:Go Short >>
5:Exit Short

Okay, sounds good - right? The computer figured out how the day developed (using a daily bar) and took the appropriate trades in the correct chronological order. The five minute algorithm confirmed the trades. Here is another example trade that looks suspicious. I have added commentary to this one - see if you agree.

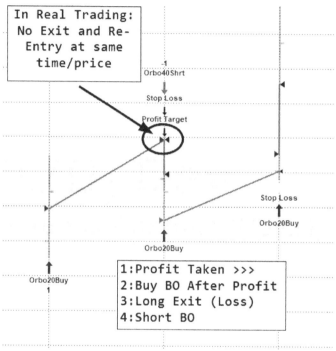

The market was beyond the buy break out stop price level when the long profit was taken. Since a new long entry order was generated along with the sell order to take a profit, the computer initiated a new long position once the profit was taken and a flat position was assumed. Placing stop orders from the prior day will automatically convert the order to a market order if the market price is greater than the stop price (in a backtest). In real time trading, a stop order below the current market price will be rejected by the exchange. In addition, in the real world you can't exit and reenter at the simultaneous price/time. Here is another whammy for you; the closing price for crude futures is based on the settlement time which is 14:30 ET. (an average of the closing range to be 100% accurate). This is what is reflected on the chart. In real trading and if this system was automated (several things prevent this particular system from being automated - but we will fix these in a later tutorial), the real price action near the end of the day is completely ignored with this microscopic view. Here is what really happened using 5 minute bars.

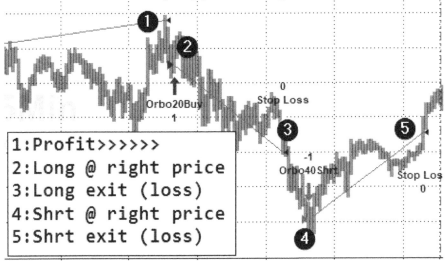

```
1:Profit>>>>>>
2:Long @ right price
3:Long exit (loss)
4:Shrt @ right price
5:Shrt exit (loss)
```

Using 5 minute bars allows you to initiate a true stop order, and then use the correct market action near the close of the day. Wow these are some serious limitations.

Look Inside Bar - Doesn't Look Inside Bar Solve All These Ailments?

Look Inside Bar is a very useful feature when working with an algorithm that needs a higher resolution data than what is currently charted. Here we can use our ORBO algorithm with daily bars and turn on **LIB.** Just format the strategy and select properties for all.

Here you are telling the computer to run the algorithm on five minute bars. This increases accuracy dramatically. Remember that good looking equity chart where I said, "Sign me up?" Here is the same algorithm across the same amount of data with the

LIB set to five minute.

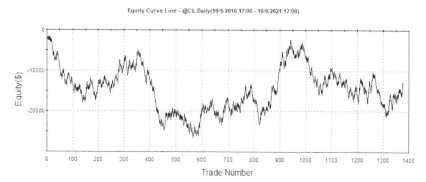

When you think you may need to know the ebb and flow of the market during the day, then always flip this switch to a five or smaller minute interval. However, this still doesn't tell the true story. Even with this feature turned on the computer still makes mistakes. Let's review the last example, but this time with the **LIB** switched on with five minute bars. The exit near the close was picked up properly, but the exit from the long profit and the re-entry at the same price/time is still wrong and therefore creates a false reporting of the algorithm's viability. If you are making decision based on the ebb and flow of the market that are event driven, then you must break down and code your system from the start to use a five minute chart. Here is a more accurate representation of the performance of this simple strategy on the past five years on crude futures.

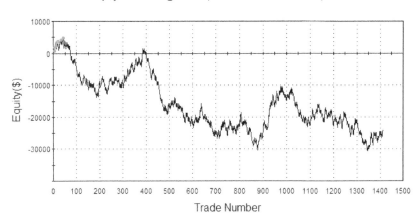

Equity Curve Line - @CL 5 min.(10/5/2016 18:05 - 10/6/2021 10:35)

Not very good! But the algorithm was designed to demonstrate the need to test on higher resolution data. There is another very important aspect of this algorithm that must be taken into consideration when trading futures: which closing price should you use?

1.) The actual settlement price that is published occurs after the close. Problem with this is you don't have this information to use at the time you need it.

2.) The close at 1700 (**SessionEndTime**). This is very easy to access from the five minute chart.

3.) The close at the settlement time. Again you can garner this information from the chart.

4.) A formula utilizing the range and the close of the settlement time bar. Something like (H + L + C) /3.

The close is very important as it determines the **BuyDay** and the **SellShortDay** in our simple algorithm. It also plays a part in the **TrueRange** calculation. The chart that was previously shown used the 1430 (H + L)/2 or its midpoint. The final version of the five minute bar version will allow the user to select 1 of the 4 options as an input.

The rest of this tutorial will provide the tools necessary to build a template for future use (pun intended). Don't worry templates will be provided for equities as well!

Information You Will Need Before Or During The First Bar Of The New Trading Session

Any daily bar based calculation such as a moving average of price or range, or any indicator such as stochastic, RSI, MACD, etc. That is if you can.

Trade signal generation before the market open. If you decide to act on the first bar of the new trading session, then know that you will be limited by not being able to use longer term daily bar indicators. You cannot mix **next bar prices** with data streams other than data1.

If you can skip the first bar of the next day, you can derive longer term indicators by incorporating data2, data3,
and so on. Can you skip the first bar of next day? If you are concerned with this you can always use one minute bars to lessen the time delay to initiate an order. Most of the time you an skip the first bar of the day and here is why: *worst case* scenario you get slipped (entry at a worse price) getting into the marke, and *best case* you skip a knee jerk reaction on a trade that would have eventually been stopped out, in other words you just barely missed a bullet. In the long run things *should* wash out.

If you still want to execute the first bar of the day or session, then know that the **openD(N), highD(N), lowD(N), closeD(N)** EasyLanguage functions do not replicate the daily bar charts, if you are using the regular session of a futures chart. These functions come close to replicating daily bars on stock data and day session charts, because none of these trading sessions cross the midnight boundary. These functions return there respective values while the date of each bar is the same. In other words, these functions start collecting data at midnight (or in the case of stocks the pre-market or the 9:30 a.m. open) and end at the subsequent midnight (stocks at the regular close at 4:00 p.m. or the post market close). Most regular sessions for futures start at 1800 and bridge midnight and close at 1700 the following day, therefore starting and stopping on different days. Based on this definition and data that includes a midnight or a 0000 time stamp you can see these neat functions will not synchronize with your daily bar chart. Now, they do work with any session that doesn't cross the midnight boundary, such as equities data and the ".D" session. We will use these functions, to a certain degree, when we get into equities trading and daytrading.

Due to the limitations of these EasyLanguage built-in functions, I created a function that takes a start time and end time and builds daily bars from the intraday data that lies within those time boundaries. The function also allows the user to use the settlement time to extract an extrapolated settlement price. These functions will be discussed later and will be available in the .ELD associated with this book.

How To Execute On The First Bar Of The New Trading Session

First off, if you just want to *back test* the idea of executing on the first bar of the following trading session, then this is doable. However, you cannot automate this scheme without jumping through a bunch of hoops. You have to wait until the end of the day, and after the market closes to calculate where you want to enter a position. At this time if you issue an order it will be rejected as the market has already closed. It would be nice if TradeStation would hold the order until the next session open, but I personally haven't found an easy way of doing this. You may know of a way and if you do, let me know I will post it on my blog with the author's name. In this same vain, executing a trade at the market close is only viable for backtesting as it will not work in an automated fashion.

Here is a snippet of code that will enable you to theoretically place an order for all of the bars (including the very first one) of the subsequent trading session.

```
if t = sessionendTime(0,1) or
(t<2300 and time of next bar > calcTime(t,60) then
begin
     if firstDayComplete = True then
     begin
         myTR=maxList(closeOfDay2,highOfDay1) -
         minList(closeOfDay2,lowOfDay1);
         upClose = closeOfDay1 > closeOfDay2;
         dnClose = closeOfDay1 <= closeOfDay2;
         stb = openTick + 0.40 * myTR;
         sts =  openTick - 0.20 * myTR;
         if upClose then
         begin
            stb = openTick + 0.20 * myTR;
            sts = openTick - 0.40 * myTR;
         end;
         closeOfDay2 = closeOfDay1;
      end;
    regCloseTime = True;
    openTick = open of next bar;
    buysToday = 0;
    shortsToday = 0;
    myBarNumber = 0;
    highOfDay1 = maxList(h,highOfDay1);
         lowOfDay1 = minList(l,lowOfDay1);
    firstDayComplete = True;
end;
```

In the code above, the portion that follows the **if-then** is triggered on the last bar of the current session. The only time the market doesn't close at the predefined session end time is when there is a holiday. Hence the additional code:

```
(t < 2300 and time of next bar > calcTime(t,60)) then
```

If the market closes early, then the session end time will not be reached, so you need to test if there is a gap greater than an hour between the current bar and the next. If there is a large gap, then you know an early halt to trading has occurred.

Since you want to be the *Early Bird* you have to prep everything on the last bar of the day. Here I make sure one full day has completed before orders are calculated and the variable **first-DayComplete** keeps track of this. Once a full day has cycled, then I can compare today's closing price to yesterday's. **UpClose**, **dnClose**, **myTR**, **stb** and **sts** are calculated based on the relationship of the current day's close and the prior day's close. Other variables such as **buysToday, shortsToday, myBarNumber** are set to default values at the end of each session in preparation for the next session's market activity. The **highOfDay1, lowOfDay1** must take into consideration the last bar of the trading session so they continue collecting the highest and lowest high/low of the session. These variables will be reset on the first bar of the following session. The next session's open tick is captured by using **open of next bar**. This value will be used as the basis for both long and short entries.

$$\triangle\triangle\triangle$$

Summary For Tutorial 14

Many algorithms need to know the exact chronological order of the ebb and flow of the market to execute trades accurately, and the only way to do this is to use minute bars.

Examples were shown demonstrating the lack of accuracy when not using minute bars.

Executing trades using the open tick on the first bar of a trading session adds a high level of complexity and also limits the use of many built-in indicators.

The code that determines the last bar of a trading session was introduced along with setting up daily variables to be used later on.

The functions **openD, highD, lowD** and **closeD** do not contain the same information that is plotted on a futures daily bar chart (regular session), and should not be used if you are trying to replicate what could happen on a daily time horizon. These functions do closely approximate the daily bar chart on the ".D" session and equities data.

Bonus: Purchasers of this book will get George's improved function that combines minute bars and packs them into daily bars using input from the user. This code will be included in one of the templates and in **Appendix A.**

Video Link to **Tutorial 14**:
https://vimeo.com/629249948/6b07523716

TUTORIAL 15 - AN ALGORITHM TEMPLATE THAT USES MINUTE BARS TO TRADE A DAILY BAR SCHEME

You probably already know that I have programmed the simple system introduced in Tutorial 14 because you saw the poor performance. The title of this tutorial might need some more clarification. I define a "Daily Bar Scheme" as one that derives its entries and exits solely from daily bar data. It is also a scheme that needs to know the ebb and flow of the market to execute signals that are derived from the the daily bar. An "Intra-Day Bar Scheme" is one where the ebb and flow of the market is used to determine entries and exits. A day trade system that monitors rallies and pullbacks would fall into this category. The first part of this tutorial will focus on markets that trade around midnight and the problems that are caused when the current time stamp is less than the prior time stamp (**t[1] = 1255 and t = 0000**). Don't worry if you aren't interested in trading sessions that include overnight data, as I will also demonstrate a template that does the same thing, but works with day sessions and stocks only. Even if you aren't interested in trading 24 hour sessions, you might want to continue with this tutorial, because there are some really neat code snippets that apply to both types of sessions.

In the last tutorial I introduced a key component of the code that gets you set up for the next session's trading activity. This template applies to using the first bar's open and also executing on the first bar (if the entry criteria is met). In Tutorial 16 we will wait until the market opens and the first bar is digested before trading decisions and calculations are initiated. I will leave it up to you to determine which template you prefer. This tutorial will introduce the first video tutorial of the Hi-Res edition, and will go over the code in detail on how I use the template to accurately program the simple system from Tutorial 14.

Code That Works With Time

```
startTime = sessionStartTime(0,1);
endTime   = sessionStartTime(0,1);
if startTime > endTime then
begin
    endTimeOffset = 0;
    if t >= startTime+barInterval and t<= 2359 then
      endTimeOffSet = 2400-endTime;
end;
```

For right now let's just work with the regular session of crude (6 p.m. to 5 p.m. : Sunday thru Friday - a great example of a 24 hour market session).

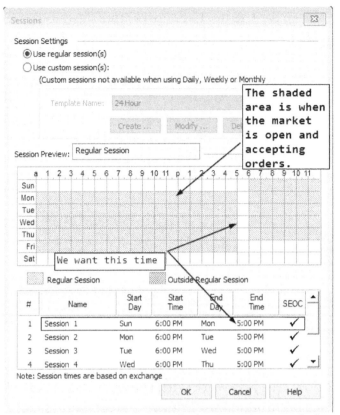

You can extract the opening and closing times of the regular session with the function calls **sessionStartTime** and **session-EndTime**. You simply pass two parameters or inputs to the functions. Here we are passing **(0,1)** which asks the function to auto detect the type of session (0) and which data stream (1). If you had multiple data in the chart you could access those times as well. If you had two data on the chart and wanted to know the open time of **data2** you would pass **(0,2)** to the **sessionStartTime** function.

The session start time and end time are are stored in the **startTime** and **endTime** variables respectively. These variables and others were declared in the following **vars:** block.

```
vars: startTime(0),endTime(0),
    startTimeOffset(0),endTimeOffSet(0);
```

Did you know there is a 0000 time stamp on a regular session chart. This time stamp represents midnight and causes all kinds of havoc when trading around the clock. Take a look at the following line of code.

if time > startTime and time < endTime then

Looks fairly straight forward - only flow into the code if time is greater than 6:00 p.m. and less than 5:00 p.m. Wait a minute! That can't happen unless you have a **Flux Capacitor.** One day I was at my local O'Reilly auto parts store and ran across one for sale. They only had the floor model and it was dented, so I decided not to pick it up. You might be able to order one at oreillyauto.com/flux-500.html (check it out). Its great for time travel, but in this case we would need to warp time. All kidding aside, the good news is the open time occurs the prior day, so it is always precedes the closing time in chronological order. You just need to add an **offset** to the **endTime** when necessary. Here is the code that allows you to compare these times.

```
if t-endTimeOffSet < endTime then
```

All you have to do now is calculate the **endTimeOffSet.** First you have to extract the **startTime** and **endTime** of the current session.

```
startTime = sessionStartTime(0,1);
endTime  = sessionEndTime(0,1);

EndTimeOffSet   0;
```

Initially **EndTimeOffSet** is set to zero. Now look at this code.

```
If t >= StartTime and t <= 2359 then
   EndTimeOffSet = 2400 - EndTime;
```

Assume the current time is 1810 or 6:10 p.m. When the market opened the time was greater than **StartTime** and less than 23:59, so **EndTimeOffSet** is set equal to 2400 - 1700 = 700. If you subtract 700 from **time** you get 11:10 (1810 - 700 = 1110 or 11:10 p.m.) which is less than the **endTime** of 17:00. **End-TimeOffSet** is reassigned this value until midnight and then it reverts back to zero.

Let us test a couple more times. Assume the market opened and 10 minutes has elapsed, so the current time is 6:10 p.m. or 18:10 and the **endTimeOffSet** will be set to 700 according to our code. If time =1810, then

$$1810 - 70\,0 < 1700 = \text{True}$$

So the program logic will flow through the **if-then** construct correctly. If time is a half past midnight or 00:30, then **end-TimeOffSet** is set to zero because t is no longer greater or equal to **StartTime** (18:00).

```
if t  endTimeOffSet    endTime then
```

Again assuming the current time is 00:30 then:

$$(0030 - 0) < 1700$$

Let's do another test. Assume time is 00:00 - midnight. **EndStartTimeOffset** = 0 since time is not greater than or equal to **startTime**.

$$(0000 - 0) < 1700$$

To accomplish what we need to do in this tutorial doesn't necessarily need this lit bit of code, but it is always best to plan for the future. You might want to only enter trades up to 1:00 a.m., and this code would help with that.

This next block of code is more housekeeping that we must do before we can get down with the actual order directives.

```
mp = marketPosition;
if t-endTimeOffSet < endTime then
begin
   if mp = 1 and mp[1] = 1 and totalTrades > value1 then
      buysToday = buysToday + 1;
   if mp = -1 and mp[1] =-1 and totalTrades > value1 then
      shortsToday = shortsToday + 1;
   if mp = 0 and mp[1] = 0 and totalTrades > value1 then
   begin
      if l <= sts then shortsToday = shortsToday + 1;
      if h >= stb then buysToday = buysToday + 1;
   end;
   if mp = 1 and mp[1] <> 1 then buysToday = buysToday + 1;
   if mp =-1 and mp[1] <> -1 then shortsToday = shortsToday + 1;
   value1 = totalTrades;
end;
```

If you have read the prior book in this series, you know that **mp** is a variable that keeps track of **marketPosition**. By using a **bar array** variable (indexable to extract historic values on a bar by bar basis) such as **mp** we can monitor when the market position transitions by comparing the current bar's value with the prior bar's value. The only weakness with the **marketPosition** reserved word and the **mp** variable is when multiple trades occur on a single bar. This is where **totalTrades** comes into play. Let's break it down

```
if mp = 1 and mp[1] = 1 and totalTrades > value1 then
   buysToday = buysToday + 1;
```

This code describes a scenario where the position coming into the bar was long and the current position is long, but **totalTrades** increased from its prior bar value. **Value1** was the prior bar's **totalTrades** value. **TotalTrades** keeps track of the total number of closed-out trades, so if the prior position was long and the current position is long, but the total number of trades increased, this can only mean one thing; the initial long position was exited and a new long position was initiated in the same five minute bar. Therefore, **buysToday** is incremented. The exact same logic applies to **shortsToday**.

```
if mp =-1 and mp[1] = -1 and totalTrades > value1 then
   shortsToday = shortsToday + 1;
```

Here is some intriguing code.

```
if mp = 0 and mp[1] = 0 and totalTrades > value1 then
   begin
      if l <= sts then shortsToday = shortsToday + 1;
      if h >= stb then buysToday = buysToday + 1;
   end;
```

If current position is flat, and prior position was flat, but **to-talTrades** increased, then you had an entry and an exit on the same bar - either for a profit or a loss. If this occurs, then you can attempt to figure out what happened by comparing the low to the sell short stop and the high to the buy stop. If the low of the bar is less than or equal to **sts,** then there is a good chance a short was initiated and either got stopped out for a loss or a profit was achieved. If the high of the bar exceeds **stb**, then a long was probably initiated. Unfortunately this is not an exact science, because we are limited by the tools at our disposal. If you see this frequently, then you must increase the granularity of the data.

Now if the prior bar's position wasn't long, and the current bar is long, then we know a buy order was executed.

```
if mp = 1 and mp[1] <> 1 then buysToday = buysToday + 1;
```

Similarly, if the prior bar wasn't short and the current bar is short, then a sell short was executed.

```
if mp =-1 and mp[1] <> -1 then shortsToday = shortsToday + 1;
```

After we are done with **value1** then we need to update it with the current **totalTrades.**

```
value1 = totalTrades;

mp = marketPosition;
if t-endTimeOffSet < endTime then
begin
   if mp = 1 and mp[1] = 1 and totalTrades > value1 then
```

```
    buysToday = buysToday + 1;
  if mp = -1 and mp[1] =-1 and totalTrades > value1 then
    shortsToday = shortsToday + 1;
  if mp = 0 and mp[1] = 0 and totalTrades > value1 then
  begin
    if l <= sts then shortsToday = shortsToday + 1;
    if h >= stb then buysToday = buysToday + 1;
  end;
```

This bit of code reemphasizes the top down program flow that
is exhibited by EasyLangauge. **Value1** is a bar array variable
and stores information on a bar-by-bar basis.   **Value1** is
only changed when the programmer changes it. Unlike the
totalTrades keyword/function which is updated internally. You
can determine the change in the value of **totalTrades** by comparing it to the value we stored on the prior bar in **Value1**. The
following code continues with housekeeping that we must do on
a daily basis, so that the information we need is constantly updated. To keep track of the current day's high and low extremes,
we must first reset the respective variables on the very first bar
of the day. From that point each five minute bar (in this example) is examined to see if a higher high or a lower low occurs.

```
myBarNumber = myBarNumber + 1;
if t = StartTime + barInterval then
begin
    HighOfDay1 = 0;
    LowOfDay1  = 999999999;
end;

highOfDay1 = maxList(highOfDay1,high);
lowOfDay1 = minList(lowOfDay1,low);
```

This code resets and updates the variables **highOfDay1** and
lowOfDay1. Since we are not using **Data2** or the **highD(0)** or
lowD(0) functions, then keeping track of this information is up
to us. Now if you just wanted to keep track of the highest high
and lowest low of a different time frame, you could just encom-
pass this code inside a time constrained **if-then** construct. You
would also need to know when to reset the values on the first bar
of the time interval you are working with. If you just wanted to
keep track of the highest high from 7:00 a.m. to 7:00 p.m. you
could do this.

```
if t+startTimeOffset = calcTime(700,barInterval) then
begin
   highOfDay1 = 0;

if t+startTimeOffset > 700 and t - endTimeOffSet < 1900 then
   highOfDay1 = maxList(highOfDay1,high)
```

I googled the settlement time for crude and found out it was 1430. The settlement price is an average of the closing range at 1430, so when the program encounters the bar that has the time stamp of 1430 the midpoint of that bar (one of three different formulas) is used as the **closeOfDay1**. Take a look at this code.

```
// if the settlementTime is missing then you have to
// make sure the closeOfDay1 is set based on the last
// bar prior to the missing settlement bar
if useSettlement then
begin
   condition1 = t = settlementTime;
      condition2 = t[1] < settlementTime and t > settlementTime;
   condition3 = t[1] < settlementTime and t < t[1];
   whichBar = 0;
   if condition2 or condition3 then
      whichBar = 1;
end;
if condition1 or condition2 or condition3 then
begin
  if settlementFormula = 1 then closeOfDay1 = c[whichBar];
  if settlementFormula = 2 then
     closeOfDay1 = (h[whichBar] + l[whichBar])/2;
  if settlementFormula = 3 then
     closeOfDay1 = (c[whichBar]+ h[whichBar] + l[whichBar])/3;
end;
```

UseSettlement and **settlementTime** are user inputs. If the user sets **useSettlement** to **True**, and the time stamp of the bar equals the settlement time, then the current day's close is calculated as either the closing of the **settlementTime** bar or a formula. If the user sets **useSettlement** to **False,** then the close is set to the last closing price of the day. Now if the data that is associated with settlement time is missing, then you will want to extract the last bar prior to the missing data. There are just two other scenarios where the settlement time stamp could be missing. The highlighted code below takes care of these two cases.

```
if useSettlement then
begin
    condition1 = t = settlementTime;
    condition2 = t[1] < settlementTime and t > settlementTime;
    condition3 = t[1] < settlementTime and t < t[1];
    whichBar = 0;
    if condition2 or condition3 then
        whichBar = 1;
end;
```

Case 1: the prior time stamp is less than **settlementTime** and the next bar time stamp is greater than **settlementTime**. For example, time[1] = 1425 and time = 1435; the 1430 time stamp is missing. If this condition is true, then **whichBar** is set to 1.

Case 2: the prior time stamp is less than **settlementTime** and and the current time stamp is less than prior stamp. For example, time[1] = 1425 and time = 800. This implies that trading closed early, and then re-opened at an earlier time the next day. If this condition is true, then **whichBar** is set to 1 also.

If neither conditions are met, then **whichBar** remains 0. Based on **whichBar** and the **settlementFormula** the **closeofDay1** is calculated.

```
if condition1 or condition2 or condition3 then
begin
    if settlementFormula = 1 then closeOfDay1 = c[whichBar];
    if settlementFormula = 2 then
        closeOfDay1 = (h[whichBar] + l[whichBar])/2;
    if settlementFormula = 3 then
        closeOfDay1 = (c[whichBar]+ h[whichBar] + l[whichBar])/3;
end;
```

If **settlementFormula** is set to one, then the close of the the settlement bar is used as the close. Which bars's close is determined by **whichBar**. If **settlementFormula** is set to two, then the midpoint of **whichBar** is used and if **settlementFormula** is three, then the average of the high, low and close of **whichBar** is used.

Algorithms that use the settlement price to determine trade entry is highly sensitive to whatever value you derive as a theoretical settlement price. I applied the exact algorithm using three different formulae and got different results for each. The first formula used the last tick of the settlement time stamp, the second the midpoint and the third the average of the high, low and close of the settlement bar. Check out these results.

EZ_ORBO_5MIN: settlementFormula	Test	All: Net Profit	All: Gross Profit	All: Max Intraday Drawdown	All: Gross Loss	All: Total Trades	All: % Profitable	All: Winning Trades
1	1	1	-12,870.00	432,290.00	-25,790.00	-445,160.00	1,420	31.76	451
2	2	2	-21,800.00	426,290.00	-31,210.00	-448,090.00	1,421	31.53	448
3	3	3	-21,970.00	426,250.00	-30,480.00	-448,220.00	1,422	31.43	447

The number of trades were nearly identical, but the $P/L and drawdown metrics were considerably different between formula 1 and the other two formulae. This indicates that you should do the research and pick one formula and stick with it. This discrepancy forced me to test on five years of one minute data to see if the sensitivity decreased. Since the range of a one minute bar should be less than that of a five minute bar, the spread of deviation should be less, right?

EZ_ORBO_5MIN: settlementFormula	Test	A	All: Net Profit	All: Gross Profit	All: Max Intraday Drawdown	All: Gross Loss	All: Total Trades	All: % Profitable	All: Winning Trades
1	1		1	-15,940.00	430,620.00	-27,680.00	-446,560.00	1,421	31.60	449
2	2		2	-12,340.00	432,810.00	-25,610.00	-445,150.00	1,420	31.69	450
3	3		3	-11,160.00	433,270.00	-25,850.00	-444,430.00	1,420	31.76	451

You would think that the exact same results would be derived by using the last tick of the 1430 bar (test 1), but that was not the case. The one minute bar generated two fewer winning trades. If the two additional losing trades lost $500 apiece, then that could equate to around $3000 (2 X 500 [losers] + 2 X 1000 [winners]) in the difference in equity. If those two losing trades were actually winners in the five minute bar test. Possibly a profit was incorrectly taken on a single five minute bar. Similar to how a daily bar erroneously reports P/L versus a five minute bar, this effect could trickle down from a five minute bar to a one minute bar. The moral of this story is it is okay to develop on five minute bars, but you better drop all the way down to one minute before putting real money on the line. Of course this only applies to those algorithms that don't use pattern recognition or indicator values based on the **barInterval**. An RSI calculation for the last seven 5-minute bars will be different than the same calculation on the last seven 1-minute bars. In this case, trade what you test and check for discrepancies. And another thing, keep in mind how tight the profit and loss values are in relation to the underlying market. Can a $1000 gain and/or a $500 loss occur on a single five minute bar in crude oil. On report days this can definitely happen. The templates presented here can be used on either five or one minute bars. Remember there aren't any **barInteval** calculations nor pattern recognition going on.

Using Our Own Variables To Calculate And Execute Order Entries

The following code was revealed in the previous tutorial.

```
if firstDayComplete = True then
begin
   upClose = closeOfDay1 > closeOfDay2;
   dnClose = closeOfDay1 <= closeOfDay2;
   myTR=maxList(closeOfDay2,highOfDay1)-
     minList(closeOfDay2,lowOfDay1);
   stb = openTick + 0.40 * myTR;
   sts = openTick - 0.20 * myTR;
   if upClose then
   begin
      stb = openTick + 0.20 * myTR;
      sts = openTick - 0.40 * myTR;
   end;
   closeOfDay2 = closeOfDay1;
end;
```

Here the code determines if there was an up or down close and the true range **TR** of yesterday. All these values are calculated using our own homemade variables. Once this information is derived, we can then get down to business and place some orders.

```
if firstDayComplete then
begin
   if upClose then
   begin
     stb = openTick + 0.20 * myTR;
     sts = openTick - 0.40 * myTR;
     if buysToday = 0 and c <= stb then
         buy("Orbo20Buy") next bar at stb stop;
     if shortsToday = 0 and c >= sts then
         sellShort("Orbo40Shrt") next bar at sts stop;
   end
   else
   begin
     stb = openTick + 0.40 * myTR;
     sts = openTick - 0.20 * myTR;
     if buysToday = 0 and c <= stb then
         buy("Orbo40Buy") next bar at stb stop;
     if shortsToday = 0 and c >= sts then
         sellShort("Orbo20Shrt") next bar at sts stop;
   end;
end;
```

Stb and **sts** (buy stop and short stop) are calculated based on if there was an **upClose** or **downClose**. Now these variables have been calculated on the last bar of the prior day since everything we need was already available to us. However, to make things easier to read *I sometimes also put the entry levels right near the trade directive codes.* This is just my personal preference. This code could easily be simplified, but I want to have different signal names for what type of day (BuyEasier or ShortEasier) that is being used to determine the entry levels. The order directives only take place if **buysToday** or **shortsToday** = 0. From this, you can deduce that only two trade entries in opposite directions can take place during the trading day. Another key concept is to check that the close of the five or one minute bar is below the buy stop and that the close is above the sell short stop. This check prevents from placing orders that would in real time be rejected. You can't place a **buy** or **buyToCover** stop below the market, nor can you place a **sell short** or **sell** order above the market. However, these orders convert to market orders in back testing. You might want to bypass checking the close relationship to the stop prices, if you plan on trading the system manually and can go to the market if the price level dictates you to do so. Checking the close price level prior to placing a stop order makes sure you get executed near your price. This is how you use intraday data to replicate what seems to be a simple daily bar system.

Now Here Is The Template For Trading Stocks Or The ".D" Sessions

If you are working with stock or ".D" commodity/futures data, then you can simplify the code considerably. The additional code that works around midnight can be removed completely. Here we can use the **highD(0)** and **lowD(0)** functions to keep track of the daily high and daily low prices. However, we are still stuck with trying to calculate the settlement price. So this block of code is still used and its up to the user to to either use the last price at the settlement time stamp or a formula such as $(H + L)/2$ or $(H+ L + C)/3$. In addition, since the **sessionEndTime** may not correspond to the **settlementTime**, we will need to check this in the block of code that is executed on the last bar of the chart.

```
if t = sessionEndTime(0,1) or
(t < sessionEndTime(0,1) and date of tomorrow <> date) then
begin
   if firstDayComplete = True then
   begin
     if useSettlement = False then closeOfDay1 = c;
     if useSettlement then
     begin
      condition1 = t = settlementTime;
       condition2 = t[1] < settlementTime and t > settlementTime;
      condition3 = t[1] < settlementTime and t < t[1];
      whichBar = 0;
      if condition2 or condition3 then
        whichBar = 1;
     end;

     if condition1 or condition2 or condition3 then
     begin
       if settlementFormula = 1 then closeOfDay1 = c[whichBar];
      if settlementFormula = 2 then
        closeOfDay1 = (h[whichBar] + l[whichBar])/2;
```

```
            if settlementFormula = 3 then
        closeOfDay1 = (c[whichBar]+h[whichBar]+l[whichBar])/3;
      end;
    upClose = closeOfDay1 > closeOfDay2;
    dnClose = closeOfDay1 <= closeOfDay2;
    myTR = maxList(closeOfDay2,highD(0))-minList(closeOf
        Day2,lowD(0));
    stb = openTick + 0.40 * myTR;
    sts = openTick - 0.20 * myTR;
    if upClose then
    begin
        value2 = value2 + 1;
        stb = openTick + 0.20 * myTR;
        sts = openTick - 0.42 * myTR;
    end;
  end;
```

At this point you are probably getting frustrated with having to keep track of the data and the housekeeping that we are doing. You have every right to be frustrated, but the good news is when you get it programmed you will have it forever and should only have to modify it every so slightly in the future.

Did you notice how we use the functions **highD(0)** and **lowD(0)** in our **True Range** calculation? At least we can use these functions and eliminate that little bit of housekeeping. Here is the same system, with the proper modifications, applied to 5 years of @ES.D data.

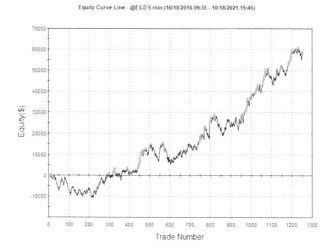

Equity Curve Line - @ES.D 5 min.(10/18/2016 09:35 - 10/18/2021 15:45)

At least the concept might bear some fruit. This is a very simple and basic trading system that has been programmed as accurately as possible (using 5 minute bars) and it might just be a foundation for further research. In real time trading 5 minutes is a life time. Look at the following example.

The first long entry was stopped out on the first bar of the trading day. And a long position was initiated on the second bar. In reality the long position should have been executed on the first bar too. In our code we have

If close < stb then buy ...

On the last bar of the prior day, the close was well above the buy stop and if it could have been issued it would have been rejected. So the market had to get in tune with the buy stop. In this example, the market retraced and we were able to get in at our buy stop. Had the market not retraced we wouldn't have gotten into the long position. If you need to you can increase resolution and drop down to a one minute bar. Here is the same trade on on a one minute bar.

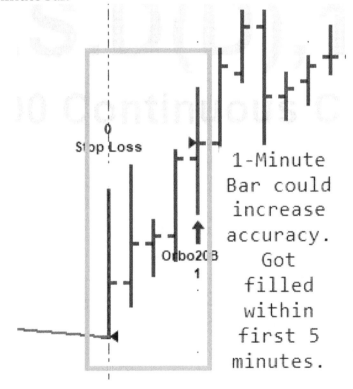

Once the first bar of the session was digested the close was in alignment (below stop price) with the buy stop order. So the order could legally be placed on each bar and it was eventually filled on the fifth one minute bar. The five minute bar executed at the same price, only because the close of the five minute bar was equal to the buy stop level. Had it closed above the buy stop level, it would not have been filled.

$$\triangle\triangle\triangle$$

Summary For Tutorial 15

Hopefully this tutorial didn't completely freak you out or bore you to death. Many times you have to plow through the boring minutiae to build a complete understanding, before moving on to more fun topics. As you will find in the next tutorial, you can work around much of the housekeeping we did in this chapter by using **Data2** as a daily bar. A somewhat generic template was presented that allows for overlaying a daily bar algorithm on intraday data.

Working with time is very important and bridging the 0000 time stamp can cause huge problems. Also having a start time that seems to occur after an end time is difficult to work with as well.

Code was introduced to help with the midnight time stamp and also a start time and end time offset was developed to get over situations where the start time is later than the end time.

Converting **MarketPosition** to a bar array (**mp**) and then comparing consecutive bar values is not sufficient to determine if a trade has occurred. If multiple trades can take place on a single bar, then additional logic needs to be used to accurately keep track of trades. **TotalTrades** is the key to formulate the code that can monitor trades as accurately as possible.

If you are trading around the clock you *cannot* use the canned functions **openD, highD, lowD, closeD**, because they do not replicate the daily bar accurately. You, as the programmer/trader, must do the housekeeping necessary to keep track of these values. The code to help with this was presented in the tutorial.

Intraday data does not hold the settlement price. You can make an educated guess by examining the settlement time and using a formula with the data that is stamped with the settlement time; three formulas were presented.

Evidence was provided that higher resolution of data does indeed provide a higher level of accuracy. The analogy of daily bars to five minute bars was used to compare a five minute bar to a one minute bar. The five minute bar can erroneously report a gain or a loss when multiple trades occur in that time frame. Dropping down to a one minute bar may provided a better picture of the market's true path.

A **buy** or **buyToCover** stop order should be above the market and a **sell** or **sellShort** stop should be below the market. The opposite is true for **limit** orders. In historic back-testing, these orders convert to market orders if the market is not in alignment with the stop. In other words, if a buy stop is placed below the market, then TradeStation will execute at the next bar's open as if it were a market order. In our code, we can compare the close of a bar with the stop level and make sure an accurate stop order is placed. In real time trading, stop orders will be rejected if they are not correctly aligned with the current market price. If you are manually executing trades, then you may not want to compare the current bar's close to the stop price, because you can quickly place a market order to stay in synch with your TradeStation.

Video Link to **Tutorial 15**:
https://vimeo.com/636590659/3bdd1b38d3

Strategies discussed in this Tutorial are:

EZ_ORBO_5MIN

TUTORIAL 16 - USING DATA2 AS A DAILY BAR

If you think you can afford skipping the first bar of the day, then the universe will open itself up to you. Here all of the indicators that you have learned to love and use are at your disposal. And don't forget automation will also be available. Since we are on the subject, we have all heard that automation doesn't mean unattended trading. However, that might be too broad of a statement. If you think you can turn your TradeStation into trading robot, then you are expecting too much and you will soon find out automation can be dangerous. If you want TradeStation to help you execute trades, then you are on the right track. If you develop a day trading system and can keep tabs on your positions throughout the day (not necessarily sitting in front of your computer), then automation is very doable. If you want TradeStation to place a profit objective or protective stop during the night session, then automation should work. But letting TradeStation apply a complicated algorithm with multiple entries and exits while you are completely away from the screen will eventually lead to disaster. If you have this type of algorithm, then its best to get a *Broker Assist* account. It might cost a little more, but brokerage houses have night desks and can execute your algorithm on their servers. So you would mirror the strategy on your computer with the strategy on their servers. Now this isn't 100% guaranteed, but its really close. If you are worried about others seeing your code or using it without your permission (proprietary concerns), then you can convert your EasyLanguage to a password protected black box or to a complete black box. Most developers thing they find the Holy Grail and are afraid of a foreign hacker breaking TradeStation's encryption. I doubt very seriously this is doable with the latest generations of TradeStation and let's not forget how important a system assist broker's reputation is to their business model. Today's brokers are highly regulated and the idea of non-sanctioned over trading of one's strategy is highly unlikely. Imagine, with social media, if this occurred the broker would be out of business the next day. They are not willing to risk their entire business by allowing someone else to illegally participate in your algorithm. It simply is not worth it to them.

Now let us test the exact system from Tutorial 14 using five minute bars for **Data1** and daily for **Data2**. You can insert additional symbols into an existing chart by simply right clicking the chart and selecting **Insert symbol...** Make sure the **Prompt for format** box is checked and hit **Plot.** You will then select the exact same symbol as **Data1** and also pick **Daily** in the **Select Interval** box. After hitting OK you should see the daily bars plotted in the lower pane.

Now that you have daily bars in **Data2**, you will be able to use that data in your strategy. If you want the close of the prior daily bar, you would use the following syntax **close of data2**. You can offset this syntax to get historical daily bars, **close[1] of data2** is the close of the prior day.. When using a **Data2**, we will not be able to execute on the very first bar of the subsequent session, but hopefully drawback will wash out with time. Theoretically this should eliminate any of the housekeeping we did in Tutorial 14, but there are situations where we still have to keep track of the high and the low of the prior day and also the closing prices for the prior two days. The reason for this necessity can be answered by one word, "*Holidays*!" A five minute chart plots every bar of market activity, whereas a daily bar will skip plotting data from a preempted trading day (most of the time). Take a look at the follow chart and you will be able to see what I am talking about.

Simple strategies like the one we are working with now allows us to do a little housekeeping when necessary. However, if you are using complicated indicators based on **Data2**, then you will just have to hope the holidays have little or no effect or you will have to create a database of holidays that will skip trading the early closing dates. If there is a missing daily bar, then the indicator's reading just carries over from the prior day. The indicator doesn't see that a daily bar is missing. In this Tutorial we will create a simple indicator that will actually write the EasyLanguage code that fills an array with holiday dates, and then implements the array into this same strategy. We then can see if skipping holidays does in fact have an effect. In doing so we could eliminate much of the additional housekeeping code.

Everything You Wanted To Know About Trading Holidays And A Lot More You Might Not Want To Know

This would be the easy way out, and in fact it might prove to be the best route to take, but I would be amiss if I didn't show the code of the hybrid strategy; the ORBO that relies on **Data2** when it's there, but falls back on different code when it's not. The code is very similar to Tutorial 15 as you will see, but I will highlight the major differences.

```
vars:
openTick(0),buysToday(0),shortsToday(0),
highOfDay1(0),lowOfDay1(0),closeOfDay1(0),closeOfDay2(0),
firstDayComplete(False),mp(0),atrVal(0),myTR(0),
regCloseTime(False),upClose(False),dnClose(False),
myBarNumber(0),stb(0),sts(0),holidayFound(False),holidayCnt(0);
```

In the **vars:** section I have added **holidayFound** and **holidayCnt**. Now since we can't execute on the first bar of the session, all signal calculations will take effect on the first bar, instead of the last prior day's bar, for execution on all subsequent bars. If time is **sessionStartTime + barInterval**, then we are sitting on the first bar of the session. Now if there is delayed open we can catch that too. If the prior five minute time stamp is less than **session-StartTime** and the current time stamp is greater than **session-StartTime + barInterval**, then a delayed opening has occurred. **HolidiayFound** is set to false and **closeOfDay1** is assigned the **close of data2**. And **closeOfDay2** is assigned the **close[1] of data2**. Pay close attention to the syntax.

```
if t = sessionStartTime(0,1)+barInterval or
t[1]<sessionStartTime(0,1) and t>sessionStartTime+barInterval then
begin
    holidayFound = False;
    closeofDay1 = close of data2;
    closeOfDay2 = close[1] of data2;
```

While writing this snippet of code I discovered that the exchanges approach holidays in two different manners based on the holiday.

1.) **Minor holidays**: the market closes early on the holiday date and the market reopens at the normal time (1800 for crude) on the holiday date - for less than 24 hour closure. These are the holidays that we will target and try to remove from the data base.

2.) **Major holidays**: the market closes early or at the normal time on the day prior to the holiday and reopens the day after the holiday. The market usually closes early on Christmas Eve and stays closed until the Christmas day evening opening - more than a 24 hour closure. On New Years and Good Friday the market will close at the normal time on the eve and reopen the following day at the evening open - 24 hours + one hour exactly.

The following code will catch a holiday if one occurs and here is how it works. Over a non-holiday weekend, the day of the week will go from Friday to Sunday or 10/15/21 to 10/17/21 or a differential of two days. If a holiday occurs in **data2**, then the differential will be greater than 2 (assuming you are using the **regular session**). This simple test doesn't catch all of the holidays. If you have an early close on the day of the holiday and the market reopens later on the same date, then this is a holiday as well. We still aren't finished. If the holiday is closed for at least 24 hours, but this doesn't occur on a Friday then the gap between the opening time date and the data of **data2** will be just one day (Christmas and New Years and Good Friday). This should cover all the bases, maybe. The exchanges can always change how a holiday is handled. If one of the three conditions occurs, then the **holidayFound** variable is set to a Boolean **True** and **holidayCnt** is incremented by one. If the market has been closed for less than 24 hours (early closing and same day reopening), then we can't rely on **data2** to provide the closing price, so all we need to do is simply look one five minute bar back in time to get the early close price, **close[1] or c[1]**. Since the daily close is carried over from the prior daily bar, **c of data2** is the same as **c[1] of data2**. Since they are the same we set **closeOfDay1** to **closeOfDay2** You might want to review this code slowly

```
if d > calcDate(d of data2,2) or
(t > calcTime(t[1],65) and d = calcDate(d of data2,1)) or
(t[1] = endTime and d = calcDate(d of data2,1)) then
```

```
begin
  holidayFound = True;
  holidayCnt = holidayCnt + 1;
  if t[1] <> endTime and d = d[1] then
  begin
    closeofDay2 = closeOfDay1;
    closeOfDay1=c[1];
  end;
    myTr=maxList(closeOfDay2,highOfDay1)-
    minList(closeOfDay2,lowOfDay1);
end
else
begin
  myTR = trueRange of data2;
end;
```

If the market has been closed for 24 or more hours we can rely on **data2** to provide our closing prices. Now that we have the proper closing prices and the proper high and low of the prior day, we can go ahead and do our calculations. Remember this manipulation only occurs if there is a **holiday**.

If there isn't a holiday, then leave **closeOfDay1** and **closeOfDay2** (they were originally set to these values of **Data2**) alone, calculate the true range by calling the **TrueRange** function with **Data2**. The rest of the code that determines the closing price relationships, resetting the number of buys and shorts and keeping track of the intraday high and intraday low is similar to Tutorial 15.

```
  upClose = closeofday1 > closeofday2;
  dnClose = closeofday1 <= closeofday2;
  openTick = open;
  buysToday = 0;
  shortsToday = 0;
  myBarNumber = 0;
  highOfDay1 = 0;
  lowOfDay1 = 999999999;
  highOfDay1 = maxList(h,highOfDay1);
  lowOfDay1 = minList(l,lowOfDay1);
```

If we have programmed this algorithm properly, the results should look very similar to Tutorial 15. Let us see if they do. First with Data2.

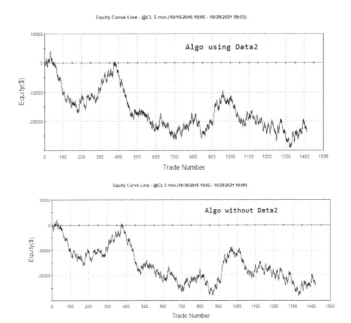

The results are very similar, but they're not mirror images. Here is an example of why the two different approaches produce distinct results.

The top chart uses **Data2** and therefore cannot execute on the first bar of the trading session. The bottom chart knows the entry point right after the open and can execute at the specified entry and exit. Here the **Data2** version side stepped a bullet as the market never rallied to the buy stop level throughout the rest of the day. Now on the flip side of the coin, the market could have taken off right off the bat and never looked back. In this scenario, **Data2** would have never got long and would have missed out on a potentially large winner. Here requiring the close of the bar to be below the buy stop level prevents the long entry at a worse price. In real time trading, as a professional trader you have two choices: take the slippage and get in synch with the algorithm with a market order or work a limit order. With this strategy potentially holding on to a position for several days, going to the market would be my selection. Now if this was day trade, I would probably work a limit order to get near the theoretical entry price. Some commodity trad-

ing advisors always try to be in synch with the algorithm as quickly as possible Whereas others try to get the best price. The determining factor is the time horizon of the trade. In fast market conditions, sometimes you are offered a gift if you wait. Waiting five minutes saved $500 in this example. There is not a perfect solution to maintaining real positions with theoretical positions. Report days have always been a nemesis to the short term trader. This is why it is so important to do your research and make a plan ahead of time. As a trader, I discovered that reports days, taken as a whole, washed out the P/L - some big winners and some big losers.

As we discussed in Tutorial 15, increasing resolution does indeed increase accuracy. Maybe the marriage of a one minute bar and **Data2** may be the ultimate solution to get to where we need to be; delaying entry by one minute and still being able to use daily bars to help calculate our favorite indicators. Take a look at how the one minute bar caught the trade that was missed with the five minute bar and **Data2**.

Generating Easylanguage With An Indicator

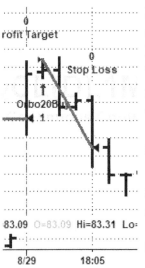

Here is and indicator that shows how you can create your own EasyLanguage and load data into an array for back testing. The output of this code can be implemented in our **data2** version to skip all entries that fall on a holiday.

```
print("holidayDateArray[",holidayCnt:3:0,"] = ",
    (calcDate(d,-1)+19000000):8:0,";");
```

See if you can see how this output was created by the above print statement.

```
holidayDateArray[ 33] = 20210905;
```

The string literal "**holidayDateArray[**" is printed first. This string includes the opening square bracket " [". The number of holidays **holidayCnt** is printed without a decimal price (:**3:0** - remember print format from "**The Foundation Edition**"?) The closing right bracket "]" follows. The **calcDate** function returns the date of yesterday (**date** minus 1 day). It is best to use this function because if you subtract 1 from 2021901 you get 2021900 which isn't a date. Why are we using today's date and why are subtracting one? The code, you will soon see, discovers a holiday after the fact. Labor Day 2021 fell on September the 6th. This fact wasn't uncovered until 6:00 p.m. or1800 on the 6th. Markets usually start trading on a holiday after the evening open. This follows a shortened trading session that opened the normal time but didn't trade the entire 24 hour or full session. Labor Day was the 6th, but if you want to skip that entire day, then the preempted trading session actually started the prior day on September 5th at 6:00 p.m. This function returns the crazy TradeStation date of 1210906, so 19000000 needs to be added. The complete output is finalized by adding a semicolon ";". This is a complete and syntactically correct EasyLanguage statement.

First I will show the indicator code, and then show how I applied it to my EZ_ORBO_5MIN algorithm, so I would skip/ignore holiday data.

```
// prints out holiday dates from daily bars
// creates actual EasyLanguage code that can be copied/pasted
// into an indicator and Verified
// by George Pruitt
vars: isTodayHoliday(False),holidayCnt(0),
isWeekEnd(False),offSet(0);
// print out the Arrays declaration in EL
if barNumber = 1 then
    print("arrays: holidayDateArray[200](0);");

isTodayHoliday = False;
// if one bar is missing and 3 day gap then holiday
// think Labor Day 2021 Friday 9/03 next date 9/07
if d > calcDate(d[1],3) then
    isTodayHoliday = True;
// if one bar missing and today is not Monday
// think Thanksgiving 2021 Wednesday 11/24 next date 11/26
if d > calcDate(d[1],1) and dayOfWeek(d) <> 1 then
    isTodayHoliday = True;
if isTodayHoliday then
begin
    holidayCnt = holidayCnt + 1;
    offSet = -1;
    // if back up one day is Sunday
    if dayOfWeek(calcDate(d,-1)) = 7 then
        offSet = -2;
    // if back up two day is Saturday
    if dayOfWeek(calcDate(d,-2)) = 6 then
        offSet = -3;
    // if Christmas back up one more day to get Christmas Eve
    if month(calcDate(d,offSet)) = 12 and
    dayOfMonth(calcDate(d,offSet)) = 25 then
        offSet = offSet - 1;
    print("holidayDateArray[",holidayCnt:3:0,"] = ",
    (calcDate(d,offSet)+19000000):8:0,";");
end;
```

Remember this code is to be applied to daily bars. This simple algorithm searches for missing bars by comparing the date difference between today's date and yesterday's date. If there is a gap of three days, then there is a holiday. If there is a gap of one day and today is not a Monday, then there is a holiday similar to Thanksgiving. If the holiday is Christmas and it falls inside the work week, then reach back another day and get Christmas eve.

If Christmas falls on a Sunday, then the following Monday is the holiday. Remember this information is going to be used to pre-emptively stop trading on shortened sessions and to also ignore the data of these shortened sessions in our calculations.

Using Your Arrays And Data To Skip Trading Holiday Sessions

Here is the output showing the holidays for the past five years on the crude market.

```
arrays: holidayDateArray[200](0);

holidayDateArray[ 1] = 20161226;
holidayDateArray[ 2] = 20170102;
holidayDateArray[ 3] = 20170116;
holidayDateArray[ 4] = 20170220;
holidayDateArray[ 5] = 20170414;
holidayDateArray[ 6] = 20170529;
holidayDateArray[ 7] = 20170704;
holidayDateArray[ 8] = 20170904;
holidayDateArray[ 9] = 20171123;
holidayDateArray[ 10] = 20171224;
holidayDateArray[ 11] = 20180101;
holidayDateArray[ 12] = 20180115;
holidayDateArray[ 13] = 20180219;
holidayDateArray[ 14] = 20180330;
holidayDateArray[ 15] = 20180528;
holidayDateArray[ 16] = 20180704;
holidayDateArray[ 17] = 20180903;
holidayDateArray[ 18] = 20181122;
holidayDateArray[ 19] = 20181224;
holidayDateArray[ 20] = 20190101;
holidayDateArray[ 21] = 20190121;
holidayDateArray[ 22] = 20190218;
holidayDateArray[ 23] = 20190419;
holidayDateArray[ 24] = 20190527;
holidayDateArray[ 25] = 20190704;
holidayDateArray[ 26] = 20190902;
holidayDateArray[ 27] = 20191128;
holidayDateArray[ 28] = 20191224;
holidayDateArray[ 29] = 20200101;
holidayDateArray[ 30] = 20200120;
holidayDateArray[ 31] = 20200217;
holidayDateArray[ 32] = 20200410;
holidayDateArray[ 33] = 20200525;
holidayDateArray[ 34] = 20200703;
holidayDateArray[ 35] = 20200907;
```

```
holidayDateArray[ 36] = 20201126;
holidayDateArray[ 37] = 20201224;
holidayDateArray[ 38] = 20210101;
holidayDateArray[ 39] = 20210118;
holidayDateArray[ 40] = 20210215;
holidayDateArray[ 41] = 20210402;
holidayDateArray[ 42] = 20210531;
holidayDateArray[ 43] = 20210705;
holidayDateArray[ 44] = 20210906;
holidayDateArray[ 45] = 20211125;
```

This is complete and verifiable EasyLanguage. Now here is how you incorporate this into your strategy. This code allows you to skip entries and exits on shortened session data or skip just entries or just exits. The most popular approach is to skip entry on shortened session data, but allow the exits to play out.

The use of deriving information after examination of the same data you are testing on is called two step preprocessing. Preprocessing data in two or more steps is a cornerstone of machine learning. In this example, we are simply allowing the data to inform us of when a shortened session has occurred and provide a heads-up when the back test is applied. Is this cheating? No. Can you automate this? Yes - if you continue to add the holiday dates to the **holidateDateArray**. In fact, money managers have used the concept of skipping low volume market data for years now. And it makes sense, because the risk outweighs the reward. In low volume markets, any news event can magnify a market event. This magnification could go in your favor. But when looked through the eyes of a risk manager the opposite is simply too scary. Skipping a trade on a shortened session is one thing, but ignoring that data completely is another. In my opinion, a shortened session doesn't reflect the "true" market, so it should be ignored. But you can make that conclusion, because you have the two templates to test with.

Here is some key code snippets of searching the array of holiday dates and making a decision to trade on the shortened session data or not.

```
holidayFound = False;
closeofDay1 = close of data2;
closeOfDay2 = close[1] of data2;
skipHoliday = False;
if skipShortSessOnEntry or skipShortSessOnExit then
begin
  for holidayCnt = 1 to 45  //45 total holidays
  begin
    curDOW = dayOfWeek(d);
    //shortened session
       if calcDate(d,1)=holidayDateArray[holidayCnt]-19000000 then
    begin
      holidayFound = True;
      skipHoliday = True;
      print("Skipping ",date," ",time," ",
        holidayDateArray[holidayCnt]);
    end;
  end;
  myTR = trueRange of data2;
end
else...
```

Searching the array of holiday dates is handled by a simple **for-next** loop. Since there are so few holidays, a simple linear search from first index value (starting at one each time) on each first bar of the day is not that inefficient. If tomorrow **(calcDate(d,1))** is a holiday, then today is more than likely a preempted or shortened trading session. The Boolean **skipHoliday** is set to True and the data collection from **data2** is maintained. Remember **data2** doesn't include *most* of the shortened session data. This isn't 100% true, because the market does close early on Christmas Eve and there is a daily bar for the 24th. Also, the day after Thanksgiving is shortened, but there is a daily bar for this data too. It is really almost impossible to handle how the exchanges handle all holidays, as their approach has changed over the years. However, we can get close and the programming code is teaching moment.

Here Is How You Control Skipping A Shortened Trading Session On Trade Entry.

```
// condition1 is the result of skipHoliday
```

```
// and the user input skipShortSessOnEntry ANDED
// both values must be true to invoke

condition1 = skipHoliday and skipShortSessOnEntry;


if t <> sessionendTime(0,1) and condition1 = False then
begin
   if upClose then
   begin
     if buysToday = 0 and c <= stb then
        buy("Orbo20Buy") next bar at stb stop;
     if shortsToday = 0 and c >= sts then
        sellShort("Orbo40Shrt") next bar at sts stop;
   end
   else
   begin
     if buysToday = 0 and c <= stb then
        buy("Orbo40Buy") next bar at stb stop;
     if shortsToday = 0 and c >= sts then
        sellShort("Orbo20Shrt") next bar at sts stop;
   end;
end;
```

Condition1 combines the user's desire to skip holidays and the existence of a holiday. If the user wants to skip holidays **and** the current bar reflects a holiday date, then **condition1** is set to true. If **condition1** is false, either by the user not wanting to skip holidays or by the bar's date stamp not indicating a holiday, then the order directive code is executed.

In the crude oil market, the number of days that are skipped are around seven per year. If you back test five years, then that adds up to about 35 affected trading days. In my analysis of the crude system and skipping holidays, the equity curve improved by around $5K. Here is the equity curve incorporating the skipping of the days where the session ends early.

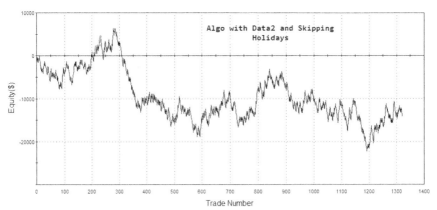

Summary For Tutorial 16

Incorporating a daily bar as **Data2** opens up EasyLanguage's vast library of functions and indicators. However having more than one data prevents the use of **open of next bar** functionality. There maybe a solution out there that can circumvent this limitation. I know that Murray Ruggiero and Sam Tennis, at one time, had a .DLL that helped with this exact scenario. Using a DLL is really a pain though and you must use an external compiler and the TradeStation SDK to create one. Also you might be able to find a solution with OOEL (Object Oriented EasyLanguage), but that is beyond the scope of this book.

Using **Data2** doesn't allow you to execute on the first bar of the next session. You can test your strategy on five minute bars or one minute bars, and determine if this delay degrades algorithm performance.

Using daily bars for **Data2** still has other drawbacks as well. The main problem is the absence of "holiday" data. An intraday bar will show this data, but the daily bar is completely missing. The data synchs properly, but it is up to you to keep track of the open, high, low and close of the shortened daily bar. The hybrid code of switching between **data2** and **data1** when necessary was presented in a template.

The code that creates a **Holiday** database was presented and a test of skipping this data *completely* was demonstrated.

The link to the **Tutorial 16** video is:
https://vimeo.com/641159384/f65e09a5e3

Strategies discussed in this Tutorial are:
EZ_ORBO_5MIN
EZ_ORBO_5MINwData2
EZ_ORBO_5MINwData2_Holiday_Array

Indicators discuss in this Tutorial are:
HolidayEZLanguage

TUTORIAL 17 - LET'S DAY TRADE!

So far, the prior tutorials concerned themselves with improving the accuracy of back-testing an algorithm that used daily bars to generate entries and exits. The five and one minute bar resolution was introduced to help monitor the ebb and flow of the daily market movement to determine precisely when and which signals were executed in chronological order.

This tutorial will introduce a day trade algorithm that uses daily bars to determine momentum and pattern recognition, but will use higher resolution data to determine accurate trade execution and additional event driven trade signals. This algorithm will be applied to the "@ES.D" as well as popular individual stocks.

This particular algorithm was introduced in the eighties and has been successful for extended periods of time. The concept is to overlay the current market activity with predefined support and resistance levels. The interaction between the market movement and the levels will determine trade entry. This algorithm attempts to garner break out and reversal alpha. Here is the algorithm starting with the before market open support and resistance level calculations.

Yesterday's Pivot - average of High, Low and Close.

pivot = (yesterday_high + yesterday_close + yesterday_low) / 3

Resistance Level 1 - the first price where the market might struggle to penetrate and may even turn back around - will be placed above the pivot price.

r1 = 2 * pivot - yesterday_low

Resistance Level 2 - the second price where the market might struggle to penetrate and may even turn back around - will be placed above the resistance level 1. It is impossible to predict exact turning points, hence the need for a second level.

r2 = pivot + (yesterday_high - yesterday_low)

Resistance Level 3 - the third price where the market might struggle to penetrate and may even turn back around - will be placed above the resistance level 2. Its calculated for the same reason as Level 2.

r3 = yesterday_high + 2 * (pivot - yesterday_low)

Support Level 1 - the first price where the market might bounce as it moves down in price.

s1 = 2 * pivot - yesterday_high

Support Level 2 - the second price where the market might bounce as it moves down in price.

s2 = pivot - (yesterday_high - yesterday_low)

Support Level 3 - the third price where the market might bounce as it moves down in price.

s3 = yesterday_low - 2 * (yesterday_high - pivot)

The chart below demonstrates how the support and resistance

levels look overlaid or projected on the following days market action denominated by a five minute chart.

This algorithm will try to capture break out alpha by going long when the market closes above Resistance 3, and only if the market opens above Resistance 2. If the market opens above Resistance 2, then it doesn't have to exert too much buying pressure to move the market past Resistance 3. This is a momentum break out going with the gap. The same concept is applied to the short side.Let's program and validate each entry separately. After we have validated each entry we can then work on the exits. One more thing before we move onto the code. In my experience its just not worth the risk to enter a trade very late in the day. You can play with what you think is the best "turn off" time, but in these examples I am going to use 3:30 p.m. or 1530.

Do Your Support And Resistance Calculations On The First Bar Of The Day And Get That Out Of The Way

```
if d <> d[1] then
begin
   buysToday = 0;
   shortsToday = 0;
   pvtPrice=high of data2 + close of data2 + low of data2)/3;
   r1 = 2 * pvtPrice - low of data2;
   r2 = pvtPrice + (high of data2 - low of data2);
   r3 = high of data2 + 2 * (pvtPrice - low of data2);
   s1 = 2 * pvtPrice - high of data2;
   s2 = pvtPrice - (high of data2 - low of data2);
   s3 = low of data2 - 2 * (high of data2 - pvtPrice);
end;
```

Now set up an **if-then** that will only allow trades up to a certain time.

```
if t < 1530 then
begin
   if openD(0) > r2 and close crosses above r3 then
   begin
      buy("R3-BO") next bar at open;
      buysToday = buysToday + 1;
   end;
end;
```

You can take trades on bars time stamped 1525 or earlier only (Eastern Time or ET). The 1530 time stamp is the time of the end of the bar. If you turned entries off when t <= 1530, then you can take takes up to 1534:59 on a five minute bar. *Remember if you use Local Time Zone in your charts, then you will need to adjust this time to your own* **Time Zone.** Notice how we are using **openD(0).** We can do this because the day session (begin time is less than end time) is compatible with these functions. Did you also notice the reserved words **crosses above**? In EasyLanguage you can use **cross**(es) **above** or **over** or **below** or **under.** Basically, you are asking the computer if the prior bar close is less than **r3** and the current bars close > **r3**. By using these words, you are forcing the market to gap above **r2** and **cross above r3**. Now remember the computer does exactly what it is told. Could the following scenario happen? A long entry when the market gaps above **r3** and the last bar of the prior day is below **r2**. The logic is including the prior day's last bar action in the trade directives.

The answer is **yes** it can. All we ask the computer to check is an open above **r2** and the a cross above **r3** before **1530**. What is good for goose is good the gander, right? Let's make this break out symmetrical on the short side. If the market opens below s2 and crosses below s3, then take a short position.

```
if openD(0) < S2 and close crosses below s3 then
begin
    sellShort("S3-BO") next bar at open;
    shortsToday = shortsToday + 1;
end;
```

Well that was easy enough and if you compare it to the long entry it will be just opposite. Open below **s3** and a cross below **s3**. Right now we are just programming the basics of the break out methodology and are not worried about any other entries today, but we will change that in a little bit. I snuck a peek at the performance for the past five years and it doesn't look too bad. Decent profit but high draw down. Remember, at this point, we only have one exit and it is at the end of the day. A profit objective and stop loss will probably help.

Now let's program the portion of the algorithm that tries to take advantage of reversal trades; trades that break out and then fail. We know this happens all the time because if it didn't, then break outs would always work and there would only be winners. Many well known traders did make a bundle on this simple strategy - a break out after some form of pattern. A break out after a narrow range seven (**NR7**) was like shooting fish in a barrel in the mid '80s.

Now we need to define a counter trend or reversal trade. What if the market opens between yesterday's pivot point and **r1** and then rallies all the thru way **r2** and then reverses course and crosses below **r1**. This would be a perfect example of failed break out. How would one program something like that? Let's put it to code:

```
if openD(0) > pvtPrice and
```

```
openD(0) < r1 and close crosses above r2 and
close crosses below r1 then...
```

Does this look right? The day opens between **pvtPrice** and **r1** and crosses above **r2** and then crosses below **r1**. On paper it looks right. But remember the computer is evaluating one bar at a time - in this case the **close** of the bar. The close cannot **cross above r2** and **below r1** at the same time. Well, what if we compared the prior bar's close to see if it **crosses above r2** and then compare the current bar's close to **r1**? Wouldn't that do it? Yes if you want the bars to fit this pattern of crossing above and crossing below on a consecutive bar basis. If you don't care how many bars occur between the **crossing above r2** and **crossing below r1**, then this code or idea wouldn't work.

If you read the *Foundation Edition,* I introduce two different programming paradigms.

CBES - the consecutive bar exact sequence paradigm
VBLS - the variable bar liberal sequence paradigm

The code that we tried to program this counter trend entry would fall under the **CBES paradigm**. Here we include everything in one **if-then** construct and expect things to happen on two consecutive bars. Well this will not work, so we need to apply the **VBLS paradigm**.

In **Foundation**, I touched upon the concept of **Finite State Machine**. Pac-Man is a good analog of a FSM - Pac-Man moves through the maze and shifts into different phases (run or chase or advance or die) based on the size of the dots that are consumed and his position in relation to the ghosts. Think of yourself as a Pac-Man and you are eating each five minute bar and based on a property of that bar, you change phases or **states**. Now let's apply this concept to the task at hand. When you start gobbling bars you are in an "initial" state. After the first bar is gobbled, then you either cycle in the "initial" state or you move to "state-1". The transition depends on the open tick relationship between the **pvtPrice** and **r1**. If you are in "state-1" and you gobble a five minute bar that crosses above **r2**, then you transition to "state-2", else you stay in "state-1". Continuing in this manner, if you gobble a bar that crosses below **r1**, then you switch gears and transition to "state-3". If you don't transition to "state-3" by the end of the day, then the machine resets to zero the following day at the open. This might sound complicated, but once you see the code and go through it, it will become obvious.

In this example we will use the variable name **stateA**, because we might want to use other state based patterns a little later. First reset **stateA** to 0 on the first bar of the day and then start the machine up.

```
if stateA = 0 and openD(0) > pvtPrice and openD(0) < r1 then
    stateA = 1;
if stateA = 1 and close crosses above r2 then
    stateA = 2;
if stateA = 2 and close crosses below r1 then
    stateA = 3;
```

As each bar is processed and analyzed the state of the machine either transitions or it doesn't. If the machine gets to 3, then all the conditions of the non-consecutive pattern has been met and an order is issued.

```
if stateA = 3 then
begin
    stateA = 999;
    shortsToday = shortsToday + 1;
    sellShort("R2rev@R1") next bar at open;
end;
```

The order to sell short ("R2rev@R1") - *r2 crosses and reverse at r1* is issued. Remember to continue using nice and descriptive signal names. Once the machine has done its job it is shut down - **stateA** is set to a value outside of its boundaries. In the case of **stateA**, it can only take on these values: 0, 1, 2, or 3. Hence, the word finite state machine. Did it work or should I ask did it do exactly what we we wanted?

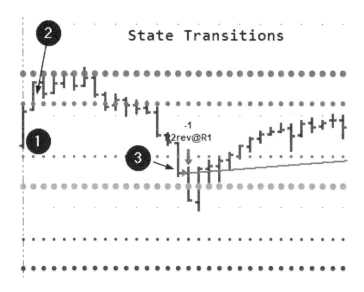

State Transitions

The first tick of the day openend between **r1** and **r2** and then crossed above **r2** and the the market faltered and crossed **r1**. So it did exactly what we wanted. Do you think you could use this form and program the "S2Rev@S1" reversal signal? The quickest way is to simply copy the code ("R2Rev@R1") and make the modifications in the existing code. This will definitely increase programming speed, but you must be very carful to make sure you use the right variable names and correct reserved words. Here **s1** and **s2** will be used as well as flipping the **above/below** reserved words.. Instead of **stateA**, the variable name **stateB** should be used. In doing so, we can have more than one State Machine working simultaneously.

```
if stateB = 0 and openD(0) < pvtPrice then
    stateB = 1;
if stateB = 1 and close crosses below s2 then
    stateB = 2;
if stateb = 2 and close crosses above s1 then
    stateB = 3;
if stateB = 3 then
begin
    stateB = 999;buysToday = buysToday + 1;
    Buy("S2rev@S1") next bar at open;
end;
```

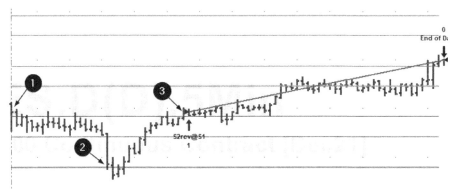

Looks like it worked. **StateB 2** occurred on a bar that also penetrated **s3**. **S3** was a penetrated, but this was OK as we didn't care how far the market fell before it recovered to **s1**.

Before continuing in this vein we should see if we are barking up the the right tree. Here is the strategy with large risk and reward ($900 and $1300 respectively) constraints (five year @ES.D with $0 trade execution costs). Looks like we might want to investigate this scheme a little further, because of the robustness of it entry symmetry.

Equity Curve Line - @ES.D 6 min.(11/4/2016 09:36 - 11/4/2021 11:15)

How about on a stock such as Apple?

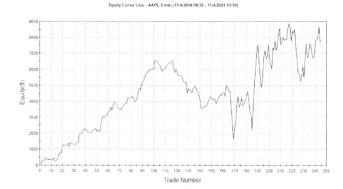

Five year test on 500 shares with profit objective of $1,500 and stop loss of $1,000. Since we have chosen the right tree, the next tutorial will demonstrate how to take this simple and discrete (hard coded) component based algorithm and convert it to a flexible framework. We might be leaning a little into the **Advanced Topic** portion of this trilogy (Easing into EasyLanguage), but a sneak peek will be beneficial in developing a robust day trading system. Remember robustness is in the the eye of the beholder. One trader may think robustness is found in the symmetry of the buys and shorts whereas another finds robustness in the longevity of the parameters selections. And yet another would interject a comment about **Degrees of Freedom** and number of trades. That last one has been argued *Ad nauseum*.

$$\triangle\triangle\triangle$$

Summary For Tutorial 17

Using Hi-Res data is really fun when working with day trade systems. The combination of break out and reversal entries make up a popular and successful algorithm. An algorithm that has been around since the '80s.

A great way to determine break outs and failed breakouts is to monitor the real time market activity as it moves through predefined support and resistance levels. A popular six level overlay that is based on the prior day's pivot point (C + H + L)/3 was introduced.

The use of a **Data2** was implemented to calculate the seven levels (support-1, support-2, support-3, resistance-1, resistance-2 and resistance-3) prior to today's market activity. The seventh level is the pivot price itself.

Four entry mechanisms were programmed using the interaction of the market movement among the seven price levels: two break outs and two reversals. The long and short methods were derived with symmetry in mind. The support and resistance levels were derived from the high and low and their relationship with the closing price, so those levels were not mirror images of each other. In other words support1 and support3 are not necessarily the same distance from the pivot price (O + H + L) /3 as resistance1 and resistance3.

Event driven (Pac-Man analog) signal generation can be handled with two different sequence monitoring/reaction paradigms.

CBES - the consecutive bar exact sequence paradigm
VBLS - the variable bar liberal sequence paradigm

The first paradigm is the easiest to code, because it can usually be handled by a single **if-then** construct. You can see this in the break out methodology.

if openD(0) > r1 and close crosses above r2 then...

However this tool can only do so much - it is limited to events occuring on a somewhat consecutive basis (a slightly better definition - a fixed bar spaced sequence). It can be extended by Boolean logic, but the code gets ugly quickly.

The second paradigm requires multiple statements and can easily be modeled by a **Finite State Machine.** However, it is limitless in its capabilities. But it requires thorough planning and outlining - it needs a finite number of states, transition logic to move from state to another and two terminus states (start and finish). Code was presented to reflect this type of programming.

A brief discussion of **ROBUSTNESS** brought the tutorial to an end.

The link to the **Tutorial 17** video:
https://vimeo.com/643965726/c406bd7589

Strategies discussed in this Tutorial are:
EZ_SuppRes_DayTrader1

Indicators discussed in this Tutorial are:
EZ_SuppRes_MinAndDaily

TUTORIAL 18 - MOVING FROM DISCRETE DAY-TRADE STRATEGY TO A FRAMEWORK

Pat yourself on the back, you have just created the foundation for really neat framework. Huh? This algorithm can easily be adapted to use different break outs and counter trend trades with very little coding. Let's see, through optimization, which levels are the best to use. First, let us start with the buy break out. Right now the criteria is simply the open of the day must be greater than **r2** and the market must **cross above r3**. What if we test, through optimization, the following.

1.) **Open > r2** and **close crosses above r3**
2.) **Open > r1** and **close crosses above r2**
3.) **Open > pivot price** and **close crosses above r1**

Before I introduce the modifications to the code (conversion from discrete strategy to a framework), let's fist see if a better buy break out component exists.

	Res_DayTrade buyBOLevels	Test⋁	All: Net Profit	All: Max Intraday Drawdown	All: Avg Trade
1	3	3	39,787.50	−4,912.50	76.22
2	2	2	27,737.50	−4,200.00	118.54
3	1	1	16,312.50	−6,212.50	135.94

It looks like option 3 generated the most profit, but had the smallest average trade. If you think about it, then it makes sense; the market has a high probability of gapping above the pivot price and moving through **r1**. These results provide enough evidence that a framework needs to be created. Before moving on take a look at this buy break out trade.

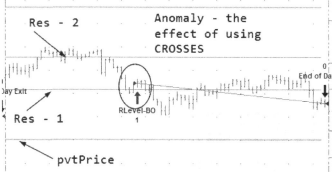

I don't think this is what we intended with the break out methodology. The market gapped above **pvtPrice** and **r1** then eventually traded below **r1** and finally moved above **r1** for the cross. Had we had a reversal trade at **r2**, then this would have reversed back to long an we would have missed out on the potential of a nice short. You can fix this by forcing the open of the day to fit between **pvtPrice** and **r1**. The short side would need to be fix as well. I did this and the results dropped dramatically. What does this imply? If the market has a huge gap and pulls back and then rallies in the direction of the gap, then you have to go with it. These are things that you must do when developing an algorithm - examine each and every trade. Now onto the transition to a framework.

A framework requires input from the user so the **inputs** statement is important. Right now we are only developing a method to choose different break out levels. The easiest way to apply different mechanisms sequentially is to use enumeration, which is the act of assigning a discrete number to a discrete block of logic. With enumeration you can also quickly optimize your framework.

Buy Break Out Levels Enumeration

```
inputs: buyBOLevels(1),
lastEntryTime(1530),profitObj$(990),stopLoss$(1300);


vars:
buyBOLev1(0),buyBOLev2(0);

//enumerate the universe of different Buy Break Outs
if buyBOLevels = 1 then
begin
    buyBOLev1 = r2;
    buyBOLev2 = r3;
end;

if buyBOLevels = 2 then
begin
    buyBOLev1 = r1;
    buyBOLev2 = r2;
end;

if buyBOLevels = 3 then
begin
    buyBOLev1 = pvtPrice;
    buyBOLev2 = r1;
end;
```

So if the user inputs 3 into **buyBOLevels**, then the third block of code will be utilized. Each buy break out consists of two components: **buyBOLev1** and **buyBOLev2**. Remember the buy and short break out mechanisms require the **open** to fall within a certain location and then the market to cross another level - in the appropriate direction. The **buyBOLev1** contains the location for the open and **buyBOLev2** is the level that must be crossed above - fulfilling the two components of the pattern. If **buyBOLev1** is set to 3 and the market gaps above both the **pvtPrice** and **r1**, then the strategy waits for the market to pull back below **r1** and then rallies past it, as we stated in the anomaly example.

Short Break Out Enumerations

Setting up the Short Break Outs is very similar.

```
inputs: buyBOLevels(1),shortBOLevels(1),
lastEntryTime(1530),profitObj$(990),stopLoss$(1300);

vars:
buyBOLev1(0),buyBOLev2(0),shortBOLev1(0),shortBOLev2(0);

//enumerate the universe of different Short Break Outs
if shortBOLevels = 1 then
begin
    shortBOLev1 = s2;
    shortBOLev2 = s3;
end;
if shortBOLevels = 2 then
begin
    shortBOLev1 = s1;
    shortBOLev2 = s2;
end;
if shortBOLevels = 3 then
begin
    shortBOLev1 = pvtPrice;
    shortBOLev2 = s1;
end;
if shortBOLevels = 4 then
begin
    shortBOLev1 = r1;
    shortBOLev2 = s2;
end;
```

Setting Up The Counter Trend Enumerations

Now the mechanism for the reversal or counter trend requires three comparisons or three components.

```
if stateB = 0 and openD(0) < pvtPrice then...
if stateB = 1 and close crosses below s2 then...
if stateb = 2 and close crosses above s1 then...
```

The user doesn't need to know this. All this will be handled with enumeration and adding one more variable. Here are the new inputs and variables.

```
inputs:
buyRevLevels(1),shortRevLevels(1);
```

```
vars:
buyRevLev1(0),buyRevLev2(0),buyRevLev3(0),
shortRevLev1(0),shortRevLev2(0),shortRevLev3(0);
```

Did you notice that there are three variables for the reversal setup? One for each component. Now all we need to do is replace the hard-coded variables with our user input derived values.

```
//enumerate the universe of different Long Reversals
if buyRevLevels = 1 then
begin
    buyRevLev1 = pvtPrice;
    buyRevLev2 = s1;
    buyRevLev3 = s2;
end;
if buyRevLevels = 2 then
begin
    buyRevLev1 = s1;
    buyRevLev2 = s2;
    buyRevLev3 = s3;
end;
if buyRevLevels = 3 then
begin
    buyRevLev1 = s2;
    buyRevLev2 = s3;
    buyRevLev3 = s3;
end;


//enumerate the universe of different Short Reversals
if shortRevLevels = 1 then
begin
    shortRevLev1 = pvtPrice;
    shortRevLev2 = r1;
    shortRevLev3 = r2;
end;
if shortRevLevels = 2 then
begin
    shortRevLev1 = r1;
    shortRevLev2 = r2;
    shortRevLev3 = r3;
end;
if shortRevLevels = 3 then
begin
    shortRevLev1 = r2;
    shortRevLev2 = r3;
    shortRevLev3 = r3;
end;
```

Break Out And Reversal Signal Fsm Setups And Trade Directives

```
if  t < 1530 then
begin
   if buysToday = 0 then
   begin
   // BUY break out trades section
      if openD(0)>buyBOLev1 and
      close crosses above buyBOLev2 then
      begin
         buy("RLevel-BO") next bar at open;
         buysToday = buysToday + 1;
      end;
     // BUY reversal trades section
      if stateB = 0 and openD(0) < buyRevLev1 and
      openD(0) > buyRevLev2 then
         stateB = 1;
      if stateB = 1 and close crosses below buyRevLev3 then
         stateB = 2;
      if stateb = 2 and close crosses above buyRevLev2 then
         stateB = 3;
      if stateB = 3 then
      begin
         stateB = 999;
         buy("+LLevel-REV") next bar at open;
         buysToday = buysToday + 1;
      end;
   end;
   if shortsToday = 0 then
   begin
   // SHORT break out trades section
      if openD(0) < shortBOLev1 and
      close crosses below shortBOLev2 then
      begin
         sellShort("SLevel-BO") next bar at open;
         shortsToday = shortsToday + 1;
      end;
     // SHORT reversal trades section
   if stateA = 0 and openD(0) > shortRevLev1 and
   openD(0) < shortRevLev2 then
      stateA = 1;
   if stateA = 1 and close crosses above shortRevLev3 then
      stateA = 2;

            if stateA = 2 and close crosses below shortRevLev2 then
         stateA = 3;
      if stateA = 3 then
      begin
         stateA = 0;
         sellShort("+SLevel-REV") next bar at open;
         shortsToday = shortsToday + 1;
      end;
   end;
end;
```

Now, we can optimize across our universe of break out and

reversal options. You can enter long and short via two different algorithms. We enumerated three different blocks of logic for each algorithm for a total of 12. Each entry mechanism can be optimized over 3 different options. If we want to cover the entire search space of our enumerations, then we can use optimization to select each different block of logic.

BuyBreaksOut **X** BuyReversals **X** ShortBreakOuts **X** ShortReversals
- OR -
3 X 3 X 3 X 3 = 81 total permutations

Here are the top ten results based on total profit.

	DayTr BOLev	DayTr tBOLe	DayTr RevLev	DayTr tRevLe	All: Net Profit	All: Avg Trade	All: Max Intraday Drawdown	Long: Net Profit	Long: Total Trades	Short: Net Profit	Short: Total Trades
1	3	1	3	2	45,213	87	-4,913	38,025	475	7,188	46
2	3	1	3	1	45,125	86	-4,913	38,213	475	6,913	52
3	3	1	3	3	42,250	78	-5,563	36,250	475	6,000	67
4	3	1	1	2	39,875	77	-4,913	33,425	470	6,450	46
5	3	1	1	1	39,788	76	-4,913	33,613	470	6,175	52
6	3	1	2	2	38,888	77	-5,025	32,438	459	6,450	46
7	3	1	2	1	38,800	76	-5,025	32,625	459	6,175	52
8	3	1	1	3	36,913	69	-4,713	31,650	470	5,263	67
9	3	1	2	3	35,925	68	-5,950	30,663	459	5,263	67
10	2	1	3	1	33,075	138	-4,250	24,613	187	8,463	52

Notice the bullish bias of the best test: Long trades = 475 and short trades 46. This of course makes sense since we have been in a strong bull market over the past five years. The average trade is OK, but think about subtracting execution fees. This parameter set does make money on the short side - about 15% of total profit. Now test #10 looks more intriguing to me [2, 1 ,3, 1]. Much larger average trade with similar draw down metrics. There is still a large bullish bias, but it is more tame. The application of execution costs would bring the two net profits more into alignment.

Finalize Framework With Signal Filtering And Volatility Based Exits

We have created a pretty nifty framework, but one thing more needs to be added. Since we are working with break out technology on a stock index it might be worthwhile to take a look at filtering trades based on volatility. Let's apply three different filters.

1.) yesterday's true range is less than the *N* bar avg. true range
2.) yesterday's true range is the smallest of *N* bars ago
3.) yesterday's true range is greater than *N* bar avg. true range

```
//volatility calculations

ATRValue = avgTrueRange(atrLen) of data2;
ATRMin = lowest(truerange of data2,nrLen)

//enumerate the universe of different volatility filters

canTrade = False;
if tradeFilter = 1 then
begin
    canTrade = truerange of data2 < ATRValue;
end;
if tradeFilter = 2 then
begin
    canTrade = trueRange of data2 = ATRMin;
end;
if tradeFilter = 3 then
begin
    canTrade = trueRange of data2 > ATRValue;
end;
```

Now here is how you can provide volatility based profits and losses to the user.

```
inputs:
lastEntryTime(1530),buyBOLevels(1),shortBOLevels(1),
buyRevLevels(1),shortRevLevels(1),
tradeFilter(1),atrLen(10),nrLen(7),
useVolExits(True),perOfATRProfObj(1.2),perOfATRStopLoss(.56),
profitObj$(1300),stopLoss$(900);
```

The code is rather simple. If **useVolExits** then do one thing, else do another. We can use the same **setStopLoss** and **setProfitTarget** with both volatility an dollar exits. All you have to do with the volatility based exits is convert them to dollars and you do that by multiplying:

perOfAtr X ATRValue X bigPointValue X currentShares;

```
SetStopPosition;
if useVolExits then
begin
    setProfitTarget(perOfAtrProfObj*ATRValue*bigPointValue*
    currentShares);
    setStopLoss(perOfAtrStopLoss*ATRValue*bigPointValue*
    currentShares);
end
else
begin
    setProfitTarget(profitObj$);
    setStopLoss(stopLoss$);
end;
setExitOnClose;
```

Take a look at these results using [2, 1, 3, 1] and trueRange of data2 < avgTrueRange(10) of data2 and different volatility levels.

ppRes_DayTrader1 perOfATRProfObj	ppRes_DayTrader1 perOfATRStopLoss	All: Net Profit	All: Avg Trade	All: Max Intraday Drawdown	Long: Net Profit	Long: Total Trades	Short: Net Profit	Short: Total Trades
1.8	0.60	38,338	217	-4,963	25,150	138	13,188	39
1.6	0.60	37,988	215	-4,963	25,925	138	12,063	39
1.7	0.60	37,775	213	-4,963	25,150	138	12,625	39
1.8	0.65	37,375	211	-5,150	24,400	138	12,975	39
1.5	0.60	37,213	210	-4,963	25,750	138	11,463	39
1.4	0.60	37,088	210	-4,963	25,963	138	11,125	39
1.6	0.65	37,025	209	-5,150	25,175	138	11,850	39
1.8	0.50	36,913	209	-5,025	27,125	138	9,788	39
1.7	0.65	36,813	208	-5,150	24,400	138	12,413	39
1.8	1.00	36,800	208	-7,800	23,575	138	13,225	39

Risking 60% of 10-Day ATR and taking profits at 180% of 10-Day ATR doesn't look half bad.

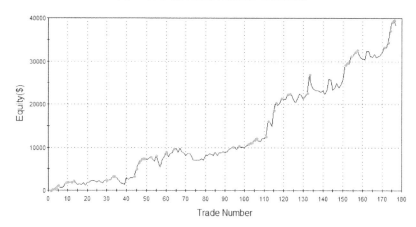

Equity Curve Line - @ES.D 5 min.(11/4/2016 09:35 - 11/4/2021 16:15)

Remember [2, 1, 3, 1] =

```
buyBOLev1 = r1;
buyBOLev2 = r2;

shortBOLev1 = s2;
shortBOLev2 = s3;

buyRevLev1 = s2;
buyRevLev2 = s3;
buyRevLev3 = s3;

shortRevLev1 = pvtPrice;
shortRevLev2 = r1;
shortRevLev3 = r2;
```

These results look great, but did we over-curve fit? One test we can do is check the strategy on data that was not used in the optimization phase. Here is the curve going back ten years.

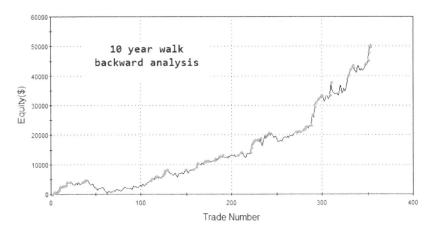

The good news is the strategy held up, but the bad news is that returns grew at a much slower rate in the early stages. Is this the type of strategy that needs to be optimized periodically? Let's think about what we have developed here. We know the strategy has a strong bias to the long side because that is what the results suggested. Our data mining uncovered this. The break out component makes it much easier to buy than short. The reversal components seem to be the opposite. To sell short the market needs to open between the **pvtPrice** and **r1** and then rally through **r2** and then pull back to **r1**. Entering long seems more difficult; open between **s2** and **s3** and pull back to **s3** and then rally to **s2**. When the bull market loses its steam, then the bullish bias should probably be tempered.

Does Increasing The Resolution Change The Outcome Of This Type Of Algorithm

If your algorithm keys off of a certain pattern based on a five minute chart, then changing to a one minute chart can have a dramatic impact. If, for example, you are buying after three ascending closings on a five minute increment, then doing the same for a one minute increment can make all the difference in the world. Momentum on different resolutions gives totally different values, needless to say. Candlesticks as well as as patterns can be completely different. With our current algorithm the entry components should get into trades earlier since it will not have to wait for the end of a five minute bar. However, a one minute bar might close at a certain level whereas its five minute counterpart may close at a completely different price. So, a trade that takes place on a one minute bar may not take place on a five minute bar. Since we are limiting entries two just two a day and only after a less than average true range day, the potential of a large increase in trading frequency should be squelched. Here is a test over the past five years on a one minute bar.

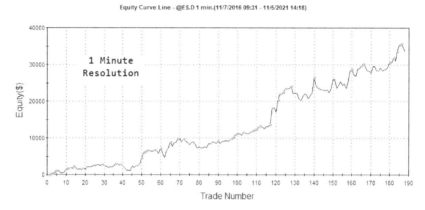

Equity Curve Line - @ES.D 1 min.(11/7/2016 09:31 - 11/5/2021 14:18)

The results look similar, but they are different. This version made ten more trades and made $3,000 less in profit. Percent wins dropped slightly, but average trade dropped more than 10%. Any time you are comparing the close of a bar against a price level, be it a prior bar or a support/resistance level then know that changing resolution changes the algorithm. A comparison of a bar formation is a pattern and patterns change when increasing or decreasing resolution.

Can You Judge Robustness By Using The Exact Same Algorithm On Same Sector Market

What is your opinion of trading this strategy on the Nasdaq? I would think it should work. I said should. The Nasdaq has a high correlation to the ES as they are both stock indices. However their risk metrics are different. Buy and Hold for the ES.D for the past five years is 103% and its double that for the NQ.D at 206%. The underlying mechanism to the algorithm should work, but the risk and reward parameters will probably need to be adjusted. Check out this optimization of the algorithm on the NQ.D.

	ppRes_DayTrader1 perOfATRProfObj	ppRes_DayTrader1 perOfATRStopLoss	All: Net Profit	All: Avg Trade	All: Max Intraday Drawdown	Long: Net Profit	Long: Total Trades	Short: Net Profit	Short: Total Trades
1	0.9	0.50	25,915	173	-10,335	22,175	120	3,740	30
2	1.4	0.50	25,820	172	-10,410	20,955	120	4,865	30
3	1.3	0.50	25,580	171	-10,410	20,955	120	4,625	30
4	1.0	0.50	25,455	170	-9,885	20,955	120	4,500	30
5	0.8	0.50	25,355	169	-10,785	21,755	120	3,600	30
6	1.2	0.50	25,345	169	-10,410	20,955	120	4,390	30
7	1.1	0.50	25,110	167	-10,410	20,955	120	4,155	30
8	1.8	0.50	24,250	162	-10,410	20,955	120	3,295	30
9	1.7	0.50	24,195	161	-10,410	20,955	120	3,240	30
10	1.6	0.50	24,140	161	-10,410	20,955	120	3,185	30

This report tells us that the risk value is very similar to the ES.D, but the NQ.D prefers a slightly tighter profit objective. The bullish bias is definitely expressed by looking at the Long Net Profit versus the Short Net Profit. I will leave further investigation of these markets and the framework up to you. This could be a very powerful tool. An area of further research could be in using Fuzzy Logic around the support and resistance levels. There are several algorithms selling for mucho dinero that uses this exact approach, but manipulates the levels by a coefficient or some adaptive engine.

$$\triangle\triangle\triangle$$

Summary Of Tutorial 18

When developing algorithms that have multiple ways to enter and/or exit trades that can be derived by a singular methodology, always think ahead and plan on changing the discrete code to a framework. I am not simply talking about changing parameter values. Entries that use the same calculations, but can use different, yet congruent forms of logic to place trades at different levels should be programmed into a singular entity. Just like we did with the the break out/reversal algorithm. We took it from a strict strategy to a tool that can test a plethora of combinations.

TradeStation's optimization capabilities lends itself well to applying different logic through enumeration. Step ping through a parameter set one increment at a time can cover the total universe of different options.

Eighty one different logic sets were investigated through the use of TradeStation's brute force optimizer.

Even though intraday data demonstrates similar fractal properties (looking at one minute chart is like looking at five minute chart), the formation of consecutive bars and their individual price relationships to each other or other price levels can be very dissimilar. In other words if your algorithm is pattern based (comparing the close of a bar to a price level is a pattern), then trade what you test.

A discussion on robustness was introduced: markets from the same sector should perform similarly without indepth optimization on the same algorithm, if robustness does indeed exist.

The link to the **Tutorial 18** video is:
https://vimeo.com/647343005/8f44dcf7e3

Strategies discussed in this Tutorial are:
EZ_SuppRes_DayTrader1_Opt

Indicators discussed in this Tutorial are:
EZ_SuppRes_MinAndDaily

TUTORIAL 19 - DAY-TRADING CONTINUED: VOLATILITY BASED OPEN RANGE BREAK OUT WITH PATTERN RECOGNITION

U sing volatility to determine entry and exit levels is still very popular today for day and swing trading. In this tutorial I will introduce a framework (don't worry we will not derive it) that will allow you to develop a day trading system that monitors day of week analysis, time based entries and accurate entries accounting during the trading day. This strategy will continue using pattern recognition to determine *"BuyEasier"* and *"ShortEasier"* days. Here is an overview of what I wanted to test and how I wanted to fine tune the parameters in the framework.

First, test the concept of a combination of the relationship between the prior two day's closing prices and today's open tick with yesterday's close. There are four combinations that I want to test.

1.) close of data2 >= close[1] of data2 and open tick >= close of data2.
2.) close of data2 >= close[1] of data2 and open tick < close of data2.
3.) close of data2 < close[1] of data2 and open tick >= close of data2

4.) close of data2 < close[1] of data2 and open tick < close of data2

You could represent the universe of these combinations with a string.

1.) "+ +" up close and gap up

2.) "+ -" up close and gap down

3.) "- +" down close and gap up

4.) "- -" down close and gap down

Using these patterns we can data mine and determine what sequence provides the days where it should be more productive to buy or sell short. Let's start right here and introduce the **switch - case** programming construct. I am going to show the code to determine the two prior day's closing price relationship.

```
switch(closePatternNum)
begin
    Case 1:
        buyPattMatch = close of data2 >= close[1] of Data2;
        shortPattMatch = close of data2 < close[1] of Data2;
    Case 2:
        buyPattMatch = close of data2 < close[1] of Data2;
        shortPattMatch = close of data2 >= close[1] of Data2;
    Default:
        buyPattMatch = False;
        shortPattMatch = False;
end;
```

Since you are probably getting pretty good at interpreting EasyLanguage, you might have a gist of what this is doing. However, the syntax might be new to you. The **switch-case** construct is not in every language and you could do the same with the **if-then**, but it wouldn't look so eloquent.

First off **closePatternNum** is going to be an **input**. Based on its value (enumeration), the flow of the program logic will change. The keyword **switch** basically tells the computer to go to the block of logic that corresponds with the value that is within the parentheses that follow the keyword. Here we just have three **cases** - **1**, **2** and **default**. If **closePatternNum** has the value of one, the **buyPattMatch** (*Booloean or True/False type*) will be set to true if the **close of data2 >= close[1] of data2** and **shortPatt-Match** will be set to true if the opposite occurs. Now if the **closePatternNum** is equal to two, then the logic is inverted.

buyPattMatch is true if **c of data2 < c[1] of data2**
and
shortPattMatch is true if **c of data2 >= c[1] of data2**

The variables **buyPattMatch** and **shortPattMatch** will be turned to off if they don't meet the pattern criteria. If for some reason **closePatternNum** is not a one or two, then the **default case** is selected; here both variables are set to false. Over the years and through different market regimes, buy and short setups have changed and this is the reason we need to data mine to determine which pattern is currently working. For many years, a static buy/sell day worked with an extremely high level of efficiency. The **close to close** relationship is just the first part of the pattern. After the initial **buyPattMatch** and **shortPattMatch** are set, we then **AND** them with another pattern relationship. When you apply Boolean algebra to two values by using **AND**, they both must be true for the expression to be true.

```
A  and B      Result
True    True  -> True
True    False -> False
False   True  -> False
False   False -> False
```

After the program flows through the first **switch-case** it enters the second. Now, since we are only comparing daily parameters all these calculations are done on the first bar of the day. Here is the portion of code that determines the final pattern recognition.

```
switch(openPatternNum)
begin
    Case 1:
        buyPattMatch = buyPattMatch and open >= close of data2;
```

```
        shortPattMatch = shortPattMatch and open < close of data2;
    Case 2:
        buyPattMatch =  buyPattMatch and open < close of data2;
         shortPattMatch = shortPattMatch and open >= close of data2;
    Default:
        buyPattMatch = False;
        shortPattMatch = False;
end;
```

This time we are switching on the **openPatternNum** input variable. In **Case 1** we compare the resultant **buyPattMatch** with the relationship of the **open** (since we are on the first bar of the day, this is the open tick) with the prior day's close. If **buyPattMatch** is true and the open tick is greater or equal to the prior close, then the outcome of the pattern is set to **True**. If the either are false then, the pattern is set to **False**. Still in **Case 1**, the **short-PattMatch** is evaluated. However this time it is **ANDED** with the open tick being below the prior close. **Case 2** works in the same manner, but the opposite logic is applied. The **Default Case** is used here as well. If **openPatternNum** is not a one or two, then the pattern is set to false.

Since this is a framework you could go into the logic and use different relationships and create your own patterns. You could also create another **Switch-Case** construct and add another leg to your pattern recognition. For example instead of checking the prior two day's closing prices relationship you could check to see if the close of the day is greater than the midpoint of the day. This is how you would set this up.

```
switch(closePatternNum)
begin
   Case 1:
     buyPattMatch = close of data2 >= (h of data2 + low of data2)/2;
     shortPattMatch = close of data2 < (h of data2 + low of data2)/2;
   Case 2:
     buyPattMatch = close of data2 <= (h of data2 + low of data2)/2;
     shortPattMatch = close of data2 >(h of data2 + low of data2)/2;
   Default:
     buyPattMatch = False;
     shortPattMatch = False;
end;
```

Now if the pattern we are searching for is found, we can move on to the rest of the logic.

```
if buyPattMatch then buyEasierDay = True;
if shortPattMatch then shortEasierDay = True;

if buyEasierDay then
begin
    stb = openD(0) + offsetPer1 * zatr;
    sts = openD(0) - offsetPer2 * zatr;
end;

if shortEasierDay then
begin
    stb = openD(0) + offsetPer2 * zatr;
    sts = openD(0) - offsetPer1 * zatr;
end;
```

Here you can see how the patterns are used to determine entry levels. The variable **offsetPer1** is smaller in value than **offsetPer2**. So if the pattern match determines it is a **buyEasierDay**, the the buy stop level is closer to the open than the short stop level. These two percentages (represented by decimal values) are multiplied by the **zatr** (average true range) and added to the open tick of the day. Using volatility and the open tick is the main recipe in the **VORBO** (**v**olatility based open range break out) concoction. However, this isn't the end of our pattern recognition chores. The success of VORBO only occurs on certain days. Toby Crabel, John Hill, Larry Williams discovered that this type of break out is much more successful if it follows a certain volatility pattern. Since we are dealing with a framework, we need to provide a template so that a user can test multiple volatility patterns. In this particular framework, there is a universe of three potential volatility based patterns.

1.) yesterday's true range < ATR * atrMult (length and mult) is supplied by the user via inputs.

2.) yesterday's true range > ATR * atrMult

3.) yesterday's true range = NR *(N)*

Continuing with the **switch-case** model, here is the code that determine if volatility matches one of our three patterns.

```
switch(tradePatternNum)
begin
   Case 1:
      condition1 = range of data2 < zatr *atrMult;
   Case 2:
      condition1 = range of data2 >= zatr *atrMult;
   Case 3:
       condition1 = range of data2 = lowest(range of data2,nrLen);
   Default:
      condition1 = False;
```

Here the pre-declared Boolean variable **condition1** is set to true or false based on which volatility comparision is currently set by **tradePatternNum**. If **tradePatterNum** is equal to one, then the algorithm is looking for volatility compression. If two, then expansion and finally if three, then the algorithm is searching for a narrowest range of the past **NR** days. The results of the trade pattern, the close pattern, and open pattern are all used to determine if and where a trade occurs. The variables **myBarCount** and **barCountDelay** are used to delay order execution. For years, may day traders felt like the first hour was amateur hour; inexperienced traders reacting to quick knee jerk reactions to economic reports. Since the demise of the pit, this is not necessarily true any more. However, it is built into the framework for your testing needs. Time is tested so you are not placing an order into the overnight gap.

```
if myBarCount > barCountDelay and
time < sessionEndTime(0,1) and
condition1 and (buyEasierDay or shortEasierDay)  then
begin
   if buysToday = 0 then buy("BBo") next bar at stb stop;
   if sellsToday = 0 then sellshort("SBo") next bar at sts stop;
end;
```

Reverse On Stop Loss

This framework will issue both long and short orders when the

volatility pattern allows. The difference between the two different entry price levels is the sum of **offsetPer1** and **offsetPer2 X**
average true range. If **offsetPer1** is 0.15 and **offsetPer2** is 0.30,
then the distance between the two entry points is 0.45 X **average
true range**. Now assuming the ATR is 40.00 in the ES.D then
the distance is **40 X 0.45 X bigPointValue ($50)** or $900. The
greatest weakness of the VORBO is the fake out break out. If
this is true, wouldn't it make sense to reverse as soon as the
fake out takes place? Great question! That is why it is built into
the framework so that you can answer it yourself. Through experience with day trading, I have learned you need to limit this
reversal within a certain allotted amount of time. That code
is in the framework as well. There are three inputs dedicated
to this entry - **reverseOnStopLoss (Boolean), reversalTimeBase
(a time), reversalTimeIncremen(a minute increment)**. If you
allow this type of entry (**reverseOnStopLoss = True**), then you
can optimize the time the signal is alive. Here is the code that
issues these particular orders:

```
if marketPosition = 1 and reverseOnStopLoss and
sellsToday = 0 and
time < calcTime(reversalTimeBase,reversalTimeIncrement) then
    sellshort("RevShrt") next bar at
      entryPrice - stpAmtDollars/bigPointValue stop;

if marketPosition =-1 and reverseOnStopLoss and
buysToday = 0 and
time < calcTime(reversalTimeBase,reversalTimeIncrement) then
    buy("RevLong") next bar at
      entryPrice + stpAmtDollars/bigPointValue stop;
```

If long and there hasn't been any shorts today the we can reverse
at the stop loss level via

```
time < calcTime(reversalTimeBase, reversalTimeIncrement)
```

a reversal order. Remember the **calcTime function**? It provides
a time value when adding minutes to a time. You can optimize
the **reversalTimeIncrement** by either incrementing or decre-
menting the input. It is best to use increments of the **barInter-**

val when doing your optimizing. If your stop is really wide, then this code is rarely executed.

Day Of Week Analysis

How much attention should be paid to the day of the week the algorithm executes on? This is a highly debated topic and one you should probably investigate yourself. Alas, even with the plethora of performance metrics that TradeStation provides it lacks this type of analysis. The good news is that with a little programming we can extract this information. EasyLanguage provides all of the components that we need to derive this analysis. Basically we need to keep track of the difference between the the profit level at the start of the day and the profit level at the end of the day. We can keep things simple by creating five different accumulators, one for each trading day of the week. Here are the variables that will act as accumulators.

```
vars:
MProf(0),  // Monday
TProf(0),  // Tuesday
WProf(0),  // Wednesday
RProf(0),  // Thu"R"sday
FProf(0),  // Friday

begDayEquity(0),
endDayEquity(0);
```

Since we are day trading we need to sample the profit stream on the first bar of the following day. The calculations are not available to us on the last bar of the day. Take a look at this code and you will see our **switch-case** friend again.

```
if totalTrades > totTrades then
begin
  switch(dayOfWeek(date[1]))
  begin
    Case 1: MProf = MProf + (netProfit - begDayEquity);
    Case 2: TProf = TProf + (netProfit - begDayEquity);
    Case 3: WProf = WProf + (netProfit - begDayEquity);
    Case 4: RProf = RProf + (netProfit - begDayEquity);
```

```
    Case 5: FProf = FProf + (netProfit - begDayEquity);
    Default: Value1 = Value1 + 1;
  end;
  begDayEquity = netProfit;
  totTrades = totalTrades;
end;
```

This time we are switching on the returned value of the **dayOf-Week(date)** function. This function returns a one for Monday, two for Tuesday, three for Wednesday, four for ThuRsday and finally five for Friday. The case logic uses the day of the week value to apply the difference between todays **netProfit** and yesterday's **netProfi** to the correct accumulator. Now keep in mind this only occurs when a closed out trade is recognized - **totalTrades** (reserved word) - **totTrades** (user defined variable). If **totalTrades** is greater than **totTrades**, then we know a trade has occurred. Once the historic data is exhausted the values of the accumulators can be printed out to the printLog. Here I pick a point in time that only occurs once to print out the analysis.

```
if d = 1211027 and t = 1100 then
begin
    print(d," DOW Analysis ");
    print("Monday    : ",MProf);
    print("Tuesday   : ",TProf);
    print("Wednesday : ",WProf);
    print("Thursday  : ",RProf);
    print("Friday    : ",FProf);
end;
```

Here are the results that were collected on a five year test of the @ES.D.

```
1211027.00 DOW Analysis
Monday    : -1312.50
Tuesday   : 10100.00
Wednesday : 8675.00
Thursday  : 16937.50
Friday    : 14075.00
```

Here the returns are fairly distributed across the Tuesday, Wednesday, Thursday and Friday. Monday is a small loser. From this analysis I don't think anything significant can be derived. Had we seen a day that was continually a loser, then we might wan to work that into our logic. However, you always want to be careful to not let your data mining skew your logic too much. This type of analysis can only be considered in a day trading framework. This excercise provided some insight into a different form of analysis and also presented code that is not built into EasyLanguage. Here is the equity curve of the algorithm that produced the numbers in our day of week analysis.

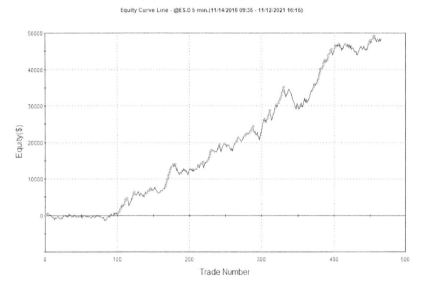

Equity Curve Line - @ES.D 5 min.(11/14/2016 09:35 - 11/12/2021 16:15)

This curve does not have execution costs applied. It does have an average trade of $104 so it could handle commission and a little bit of slippage. If you sum up the results of the day of week analysis it will be equal to the end value of the curve.

Programming Our Own Trade Management

In our prior tutorial we utilized the built-in **setStopLoss** and **setProfitTarget** functions. However, this time we are actually entering a trade if a loss occurs during a certain portion of the trading day, so we will need to handle that portion of the trade managment ourselves. Here is the final trade management logic for this framework. Just like the framework we developed in the prior tutorial, the ability to switch between pure dollar or volatility based losses and profits is encoded into the logic.

```
loss$ = stopLoss$;
prof$ = profitObj$;
if useVolExits then
begin
    loss$ = perOfATRStopLoss * zatr * bigPointValue;
    prof$ = perOfATRProfObj * zatr * bigPointValue;
end;

if marketPosition = 1 and reverseOnStopLoss and
sellsToday = 0 and
time < calcTime(reversalTimeBase,reversalTimeIncrement) then
    sellshort("RevShrt") next bar at
        entryPrice - loss$/bigPointValue stop;
if marketPosition =-1 and reverseOnStopLoss and
buysToday = 0 and
time < calcTime(reversalTimeBase,reversalTimeIncrement) then
    buy("RevLong") next bar at
        entryPrice + loss$/bigPointValue stop;

if marketPosition = 1 then
    sell("LongXit") next bar at
        entryPrice - loss$/bigPointValue stop;
if marketPosition =-1 then
    buytocover("ShrtXit") next bar at
        entryPrice + stopLoss$/bigPointValue stop;
if marketPosition = 1 then
    sell("LongProf") next bar at
        entryPrice + prof$/bigPointValue limit;
if marketPosition =-1 then
    buytocover("ShrtProf") next bar at
        entryPrice - prof$/bigPointValue limit;
```

Once the user decides on using either dollar or volatility based exits, the code converts volatility to dollars if necessary. Armed with the correct dollar based profit and stop levels, the code instructs TradeStation to execute at the corresponding levels. Here we are doing our own trade management using the **entryPrice** as the basis of our calculations.

Tread Lightly - Danger Ahead

3/6/2020 10:35	BBo	$2,896.25	$0.00	1	($2,775.00)
3/6/2020 14:50	SBo	$2,840.75		($2,775.00)	$19,587.50
3/6/2020 14:50	SBo	$2,840.75	$0.00	1	($3,700.00)
3/6/2020 16:00	ShrtXit	$2,914.75		($3,700.00)	$15,887.50
		$2,673.25	$0.00	1	($2,950.00)
		$2,732.25		($2,950.00)	$12,937.50
		$2,732.25	$0.00	1	($3,925.00)
		$2,653.75		($3,925.00)	$9,012.50
		$2,468.25	$0.00	1	($3,975.00)
		$2,547.75		($3,975.00)	$5,037.50
		$2,547.75	$0.00	1	($4,637.50)
3/12/2020 13:45	LongXit	$2,455.00		($4,637.50)	$400.00
3/19/2020 09:45	SBo	$2,270.50	$0.00	1	($5,487.50)
3/19/2020 11:40	BBo	$2,380.25		($5,487.50)	($5,087.50)
3/19/2020 11:40	BBo	$2,380.25	$0.00	1	($2,562.50)
3/19/2020 16:15	End of Day Exit	$2,329.00		($2,562.50)	($7,650.00)
3/23/2020 09:45	SBo	$2,167.00	$0.00	1	$62.50
3/23/2020 16:15	End of Day Exit	$2,165.75		$62.50	($7,587.50)
3/25/2020 09:45	BBo	$2,427.25	$0.00	1	($975.00)
3/25/2020 16:15	End of Day Exit	$2,407.75		($975.00)	($8,562.50)

> Using adaptive parameters on VOL is great, but be very, very careful!

Check yourself before you wreck yourself. During the genesis of the Covid Pandemic the markets went completely wild. Volatility was off the map and any algorithm using volatility for entry and/or exits had to be tempered because even if the the risk/rewared ratios stayed consistent the max loss to account size ratio was completely out of whack. One way to combat these **Black Swan** events is to only allow volatility friendly trading environments. In other words, only trade when volatility is below a certain level. You can also decouple the connection between entry and exit levels. This strategy uses the same ATR calculation for entries as it does for exits. It might be smart to have two seperate calculations.

This is great programming because we are doing everything ourselves, but keep in mind we will not be able to execute on the **same bar of entry**. The only way to do this is to use the built in **setStopLoss** and **setProfitTarget** functions.

Have You Heard Trailing Stops Are Better Than Profit Targets?

In many cases, the answer to this questions is yes. However, it depends on your time horizon. If you are trading a longer trend following system that needs to maximize as much profit as possible on a winning trade, then a trailing stop seems to perform better. Now on a day trade basis I don't know if this is the case always. But you should answer this question yourself. And you should know how to program it as well. EasyLanguage has a built in **SetPercentTrailing** mechanism, but I haven seen it abused so often that I prefer to program this type of exit from scratch. If you are unfamiliar with this exit, let me explain it. When using a trailing stop you are pulling your exit up (if long) as the market moves in a favorable direction and magnitude. Once the market exhausts the move and starts to pull back, you get out. Theoretically, this should work better than a pure profit objective, because you are letting the market run. In trend following algorithm a positive move can be tremendous. When you are day trading you have to deal with time decay and this limits potential profit. The percent trailing stop works with two inputs: a threshold in dollars and a percentage amount that you are willing to give up in case of a retracement. Let us assume you only want this exit to kick in once a $250 favorable position is established and you want to to risk 25% of max position profit; if the maximum position profit is $1000, then you will lock in $750. Follow this scenario, the market is very friendly and it provides a $2000 favorable move, had you only used a $1000 profit objective, then you would have left $1000 on the table. However, had you used a $250 threshold and $25% trailing stop you would have collected $1500 (75% of $2000 - you risked 25% of $2000 or $500.) How do you program such a thing - it is quite simple once you break it down. Heres the code - see if you can figure it out before I explain it.

```
if useTrailPercentStop then
begin
        if marketPosition = 1 then
    begin
      if maxPositionProfit > trailPercentThresh$ then
        sell("LongTrail") next bar at
            entryPrice + (1-trailPercent) *
```

```
              maxPositionProfit/bigPointValue stop;
        end;
        if marketPosition = -1 then
        begin
          if maxPositionProfit > trailPercentThresh$ then
            buyToCover("ShortTrail") next bar at
                entryPrice - (1-trailPercent) *
                maxPositionProfit/bigPointValue stop;
        end;
    end
```

The key to this logic is in calculating the exit price based on **max-PositionProfit**. This reserved word tracks the trade and records the most favorable maximum excursion - either long or short. This is a great function because it keeps us from having to do the tracking. Since **maxPositionProfit** is in dollars we will need to convert it to points. If market position is long and **maxPosition-Profit** is greater than the threshold, then a stop order is placed on each bar at:

entryPrice + (1 - trailPercent) * maxPositionProfit/bigPointValue

Remember the percentage in the calculation is the amount we want to risk of the maximum position profit. So, we need to subtract the percentage from 1 and multiply that difference by the **maxPositionProfit** in points not dollars and add it to the **entryP-rice**. As the max profit increases so does the exit price. And the stop never goes lower - its a *ratcheting type* stop. If market position is short, then the same calculation is used but instead of adding the **(1 - trailPercent) X maxPositionProfit** in points to the **entryPrice** we subtract it. Here is an example using $750 as the threshold and risking 50% of max profit.

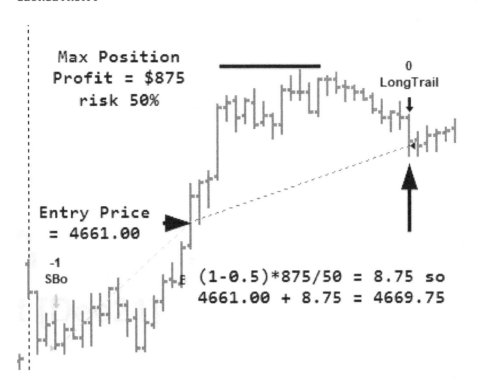

```
Max Position
Profit = $875
   risk 50%


Entry Price
 = 4661.00

  -1
  SBo
```

0
LongTrail

(1-0.5)*875/50 = 8.75 so
4661.00 + 8.75 = 4669.75

Here the market first sold off and pulled us into a short break out (SBo), but reversed quickly and got us long at 4661.00. The market continued to rally and quickly broke through the $750 threshold and pushed all the way up to a level equivalent to $875 in open trade profit. The market then started to falter and $437.50 was locked in.

Here is the risk of using a trailing stop. Had we held our position the profit would have ended being more than $1000. This is a trade off; would you rather say I took a $475 profit, but left $600 on the table or I took home a loss. Don't let the fallacy of this logic convince you 100%. If you take full losses and only partial wins, then you equity curve will definitely wilt. The key is to find the partial wins that keep the equity moving upward. Here is the best equity curve I could come up with over the past five years. Remember no execution costs were applied.

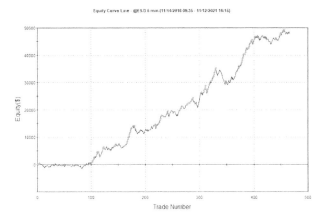

Equity Curve Line - @ES.D 6 min.(11/14/2016 09:35 - 11/12/2021 16:15)

Using these inputs.

	Value
profitObj$	1320
stopLoss$	900
useVolExits	False
perOfATRProfObj	0.6
perOfATRStopLoss	0.6
useTrailPercentStop	True
trailPercentThresh$	750
trailPercent	0.5
barCountDelay	1
offsetPer1	.15
offsetPer2	.3
tradePatternNum	1
closePatternNum	1
openPatternNum	1
atrLen	10
atrMult	1
nrLen	7
reverseOnStopLoss	True
reversalTimeBase	1100
reversalTimeIncrement	70

The profitObj$ was increased because of using the trailing percent stop of $750 and 50%. Using a small range set up with closePatternNum of 1 and openPatternNum of 1 and allowing a reversal entry on a $900 loss up to seventy minutes after 1100 a.m. proved to be quit successful. The average trade was around $110 and 47% of trades were on the short side. Shorts provided 1/3 of the total profit - not bad for such a bull market. Also keep in mind these results are the consequence of our data mining expedition. Will this type of equity growth continue into the future. Depends on the market and the robustness of our parameter selection.

ΔΔΔ

Summary Of Tutorial 19

This tutorial turned out to be rather large due to all the information that was covered. Here is a quick summary.

VORBO - volatility based open range break out is still an effective approach to day trading. The U.S. still wakes up ready to trade. However, pattern recognition must be used to filter out the days that are fraught with fake out break outs

A complete VORBO framework was presented that allows the user to customize there own algorithms.
1.) close to close patterns
2.) open tick to price close patterns
3.) break out amounts
4.) protective stops and profit objectives (dollars and range based)
5.) percent trailing stops with custom thresholds and percents
6.) time based reversal entries
Code was presented that can help the user determine if Day Of Week analysis would be appropriate to use in their algorithms.

Examples of volatility based stops where disaster can occur very quickly were presented.

Trade management logic and code was presented as alternatives to **SetStopLoss**, **SetProfitTarget**, and **SetPercentTrailing**.

Two very important and useful reserved words were introduced and utilized. **MaxPositionProfit and TotalTrades** - these keywords provide the tools to build much more sophisticated applications such as keeping track of the last trade profit and creating a ratcheting percent trailing stop.

The link to the **Tutorial 19** video is:
https://vimeo.com/652907344/b9e2a51370

Strategies discussed in this Tutorial are:

EZ_Vorbo_wPatterns

TUTORIAL 20 - PYRAMIDING WITH CAMARILLA

The Camarilla Equation was by created by Nick Scott, a bond day trader, in 1989. The equation uses just yesterday's price action to project eight support/resistance price levels onto today's trading action. These levels, or advisers, as the name of the equation suggests provides the necessary overlay to help predict turning points as well as break outs. Going through many charts with the Camarilla indicator overlay it is surprising how many times the market does in fact turn at one of these eight price levels. The equations that generate the support/resistance levels are mathematically simple.

Resistance #4 = Close + Range * 1.1/ 2 – Top Line Working Down
Resistance #3 = Close + Range * 1.1/4
Resistance #2 = Close + Range * 1.1/6
Resistance #1 = Close + Range * 1.1/12
Support #1 = Close - Range * 1.1/12
Support #2 = Close - Range * 1.1/6
Support #3 = Close - Range * 1.1/4
Support #4 = Close - Range * 1.1/2–Bottom Line

Should I Use Data2 For Calculations

Since the Camarilla levels only need the prior day's information (High and Low and Close) you don't necessarily need to use a daily bar for Data2. However, if you do use the **HighD, LowD, CloseD** functions then you will get different levels and it will be difficult to incorporate longer term daily bar indicators. In this tutorial, I chose to use **Data2** because I wanted to calculate a longer term average true range metric.

This tutorial is presented as a framework just like the the prior tutorial and it borrows a bunch of code from Tutorial 18, but several new topics are introduced. The most important of course is the concept of pyramiding. Here is an example of our objective for this tutorial.

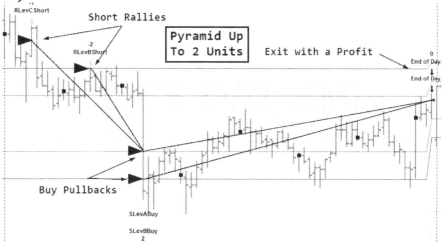

In this example, short positions are entered when the market rallies to resistance levels two and three and long entries are entered on pullbacks at supports levels two and three. We will only be entering counter trend trades in the following examples. I might need to explain rallies and pullbacks - to enter short the market must be trading above the entry price level and the market needs to be trading below the entry price for long entries. In other words, entries will be entered into the market via **limit** orders. Remember you must be very careful when using limit orders. You should always stress your algorithm out as much as possible during the back test. If you have read the *Foundation* edition, then you know that I like to force market action to penetrate the limit price before an execution occurs. Can you fill a limit order at the limit price if it is touched? Sometimes, but I guarantee a lot less frequently than you might think. So here is equity curve of our Camarilla Pyramiding framework *(pure*

counter trend) if you allow limit orders to be filled if touched.

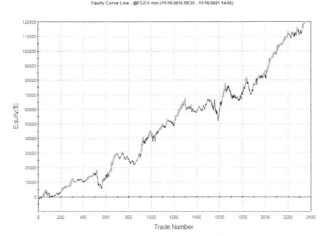

This looks almost too good to be true, but we know its not because of the draw down values. However, the numbers are exaggerated or best case scenario. Whenever you can buy the exact high or short the exact low of a bar, you will almost always reap a benefit. Here is the equity curve where we force the market to trade through the limit price (no commission over the past five years.)

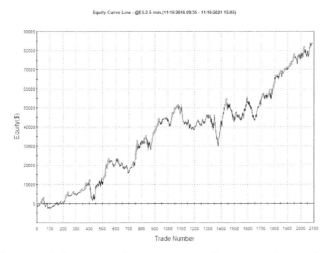

Profit dropped $36K and average trade went from $51 to $40. Now this is worst case scenario - you may get filled if the market just touches your limit order. Also keep in mind, theoretically, there should be zero slippage. Here is why you get the difference. If the market just touches your limit price and immediately turns around and you make a profit this is a winning trade you didn't receive if you force the market to trade through the limit. If the market trades through the limit, both limit order requirements are met and you are susceptible to taking a loss. So you will miss out on some winners and take all the losers. In this analysis there was a difference of 217 winners in favor of the market if touched test and 47 losers in favor of the market penetration test. So, 170 additional winners and that makes all the difference in the world. The equity curves are intriguing enough, but the code for this framework is really neat too.

Step 1: Create The Camarilla Indicator

Since I made the decision to use **Data2** in the framework, its only logical to do so in the indicator. Whenever you can create a complimentary indicator to a trading algorithm, do so, because it will help with programming and debugging. Here is the code for the indicator.

```
vars: minTick(0);
R4 = close of data2 + (high of data2-low of data2) * 1.1 / 2;
R3 = close of data2 + (high of data2-low of data2) * 1.1/4;
R2 = close of data2 + (high of data2-low of data2) * 1.1/6;
R1 = close of data2 + (high of data2-low of data2) * 1.1/12;
S1 = close of data2 - (high of data2-low of data2) * 1.1/12;
S2 = close of data2- (high of data2-low of data2) * 1.1/6;
S3 = close of data2- (high of data2-low of data2) * 1.1/4;
S4 = close of data2- (high of data2-low of data2) * 1.1/2;


minTick = minMove / priceScale;
//round down to the nearest tick
R1 = R1 - (mod(R1,minTick));
R2 = R2 - (mod(R2,minTick));
R3 = R3 - (mod(R3,minTick));
R4 = R4 - (mod(R4,minTick));


//round up to the nearest tick
S4 = S4 + (minTick-mod(S4,minTick));
S3 = S3 + (minTick-mod(S3,minTick));
S2 = S2 + (minTick-mod(S2,minTick));
```

```
S1 = S1 + (minTick-mod(S1,minTick));

plot1(R4,"R4");
plot2(R3,"R3");
plot3(R2,"R2");
plot4(R1,"R1");
plot8(S4,"S4");
plot7(S3,"S3");
plot6(S2,"S2");
plot5(S1,"S1");
```

The math should look familiar; it basically replicates the calculations that I presented at the start of this tutorial. Since we are dealing with price levels with Camarilla overlay, we should make sure they are adjusted to factors of the **minMove**. Here the @ES.D ticks in quarters or 0.25. If your calculation outputs a price like 4701.17 and you want to place an order at this price, TradeStation will accept it, but you will executed at a price that ends is 0.25. Since we are going to be working with limit orders we should only issue accurate prices.

Since the performance deteriorated so much by forcing the price to push through the limit price, I figured rounding down the buy limit and rounding up the sell short limit might off set a portion this loss and it did. Doing the opposite generated quite a few less trades and many of those trades were winners - so the equity curve grew at a slower rate by rounding up/rounding down instead of rounding down/rounding up. Here is the math behind the rounding up and down to the nearest tick.

(tp) test price = 4107.18
minTick = minMove/priceScale = 0.25

<u>Rounding Up</u>
```
tp = tp + (minTick-mod(tp,minTick));
tp = 4107.18 + (0.25 - 0.18)
tp = 4107.18 + 0.07 = 4107.25
```

<u>Rounding Up</u>
```
tp = tp - (mod(tp,minTick));
tp = 4107.18 - 0.18 = 4107.00
```

In rounding up you add **tp** to the difference between the **minTick** and the **mod** (*modulus or remainder*) of dividing **tp** (test price) by **minTick** (0.25)

4107.18 / 0.25 =16,428.<u>72</u> --> 0.72 * 0.25 = 0.18
4107.18 + (0.25 -0.18) = 4107.25

rounding down you simply subtract the remainder from the test price

4107.18 - 0.18 = 4107

You will need eight plots for this indicator. I like to color the opposite levels the same color. S4 and r4 are red, s3 and r3 are blue, and so on. These exact calculations are copied over into the strategy-framework.

Track And Record The Path The Market Travels During The Trading Day

In Tutorials 17 and 18 we enumerated the levels where we wanted to execute break out and reversal trades. In this algorithm we will continue to use enumeration, but will introduce a method of tracking and recording the market as it crosses the different Camarilla levels with our own special grammar (language structure). That sounded a little advanced, didn't it? I use a very simplistic grammar that is stored in a single string, so don't worry.

String Manipulation And Concatentaion - Two Very Poweful Tools

EasyLanguage allows you to add strings. Here is an example.

```
aStr = "Dogs";
bStr = " ";
cStr = "chase";
```

```
dStr = "cats";
aStr + bStr + cStr + bStr + dStr = "Dogs chase cats"
```

Along with concatenation, EasyLanguage offers a nice library of string functions.

```
aStr = "abc123";
rightStr(aStr,3) = "123"
leftStr(aStr,3) = "abc"
inStr(aStr,"123") = 4
strLen(aStr) = 6
```

You can extract *N* characters (a string is a list of characters) from either the right or left side, locate a substring inside of a string, and deteremine the string length. In this tutorial we will be using **inStr** and **strLen** functions.

A string is a form of a stack (a data type). You can chronologic-ally add or stack information to a string and its history will be available to you until you clear it. A string variable has a finite length, but don't worry we will only be using a portion of its maximum capacity. Here is the code the records the path of the market during the trading day using the Camarilla as bench-marks or mileposts.

```
if waitBar > 3 then
begin
    if h crosses above r1 then thePath = thePath + "+r1";
    if h crosses above r2 then thePath = thePath + "+r2";
    if h crosses above r3 then thePath = thePath + "+r3";
    if h crosses above r4 then thePath = thePath + "+r4";
    if h crosses above s1 then thePath = thePath + "+s1";
    if h crosses above s2 then thePath = thePath + "+s2";
    if h crosses above 23 then thePath = thePath + "+s3";
    if h crosses above s4 then thePath = thePath + "+s4";

    if l crosses below r1 then thePath = thePath + "-r1";
    if l crosses below r2 then thePath = thePath + "-r2";
    if l crosses below r3 then thePath = thePath + "-r3";
    if l crosses below r4 then thePath = thePath + "-r4";
    if l crosses below s1 then thePath = thePath + "-s1";
    if l crosses below s2 then thePath = thePath + "-s2";
    if l crosses below s3 then thePath = thePath + "-s3";
    if l crosses below s4 then thePath = thePath + "-s4";
end;
```

Here the string variable **thePath** is reset to null/empty or "" on the first bar of the day. When the number of bars surpasse **wait-Bars**, then the recording begins.

`if h crosses above r1 then thePath = thePath + "+r1";`

If the high of the bar **crosses above r1** the string "+r1" is added to the path. This string represents the direction and the level the market crossed the level. The "+" indicators crossed above and "r1" indicates which level was crossed. The string "-r1" indicates the market crossed below r1. Notice we are using the **high** and **low** of the bar to determine crossings.

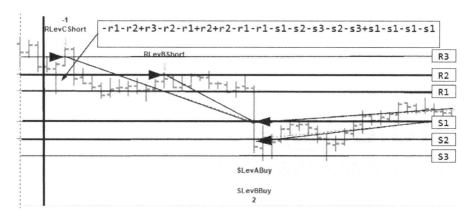

The market first crosses below **r1** and **r2** (on same bar) and then above **r3**. You can follow along with the crossings and align them with a string. Remember only a crossing counts - meaning that the high must be below the level on the prior bar and above the current bar (+crossing) or the low of the prior bar must be above the level and the current low is below the level (-crossing). Notice the wide bar in the middle of the chart - the market lows cross below **r1, s1, s2, s3**. After the market dithers around **s2** and **s3** it finally crosses above **s1**. Keep remembering this path representation is constrained to crossings. I did this because we will be entering all trades on limits and the number of entries will be

105

constrained as well. I am really only concerned with a certain portion of the path. If limit orders are used and a market crosses a level that aligns with a limit price, then I can examine the path string, on a historic basis, to see if that certain level has already been crossed. If it has, then I skip the trade, because a trade should have already occurred at that level.

```
if time < lastEntryTime and waitBar > 3 and canTrade then
begin
    if inStr(thePath,"-s1" = 0 and l > s1 and
    buysToday < maxLongEntries then
        buy("SLevABuy") numSharesCons shares next bar at s1 limit;

    if inStr(thePath,"-s2") = 0 and l > s2 and
    buysToday < maxLongEntries then
        buy("SLevBBuy") numSharesCons shares next bar at s2 limit;

    if inStr(thePath,"-s3") = 0 and l >s3 and
    buysToday < maxLongEntries then
        buy("SLevCBuy") numSharesCons shares next bar at s3 limit;

    nsc = numSharesCons; // short variable name for numSharesCons

    if inStr(thePath,"+r1") = 0 and h < r1 and
    shortsToday < maxShortEntries then
        sellShort("RLevAShort") nsc shares next bar at r1 limit;

    if inStr(thePath,"+r2") = 0 and h < r2 and
    shortsToday < maxShortEntries then
        sellShort("RLevAShort") nsc shares next bar at r2 limit;

    if inStr(thePath,"+r3") = 0 and h < r3 and
    shortsToday < maxShortEntries then
        sellShort("RLevCShort") nsc shares next bar at r3 limit;
```

If the time is within the time constraints and **canTrade** is true then orders can be placed. Let us unpack the very first trade directive.

```
1.) if inStr(thePath,"-s1") = 0 //first time here
2.) if low > s1
3.) if buysToday < maxLongEntries
4.) place buy limit order at s1
```

If "-s1" is not found in the **thePath** string then we know that this level has yet to be crossed. If the low of the current bar is greater than s1, then a valid limit order can be placed as long as **buysToday < maxLongEntries**. Had "-s1" been in **thePath**, then the **inStr** function would have returned a value greater than 0. Once the market crosses below **s1**, then the string "-s1" will be added to **thePath** and a long position will be established at **s1** on a limit. Once a trade is established at **s1** and "-s1" is added to **thePath** string, this block of code will not be executed for the rest of the day. Let us unpack the second trade directive to drive this home.

```
1.) if inStr(thePath," s2")   0
2.) if low   s2
3.) if buysToday   maxLongEntries
4.) place buy limit order at s2
```

If "-s2" (**cross below s2**) has not been visited and the other Boolean tests are true, then an additional position is added at **s2**. Remember you have to turn pyramiding on in the **Format Strategies:Properties for All: General tab**. The rest of the trade directives follow this exact form or template for entering long and short trades.

So far we have covered the logic that rounds up or down to the nearest tick, builds a string that reflects the path the market travels during the day and also the logic that instructs TradeStation when and where to execute trades. The marriage of the path string with the trade directives is very important. However, the other logic that is programmed in this framework is nearly as important.

Counting Entries On A Pyramid Basis

You can control the number of times an algorithm pyramids by changing the maximum number of entry orders in the **Proper-

ties For All dialog. However, if you want to optimize this you will need to come up with the logic that keeps track of every time an entry (original and add on) occurs. Check this code out.

```
mp = marketPosition;
if mp[1] <> 1 and mp = 1 then
    buysToday = buysToday + currentShares;
if mp[1] = mp and mp = 1 and currentShares > curShares then
    buysToday = buysToday + currentShares - curShares;
f mp[1] <>-1 and mp = -1 then
    shortsToday = shortsToday + currentShares;
if mp[1] = -1 and mp = -1 and currentShares > curShares then
    shortsToday = shortsToday + currentShares - curShares;
```

Even if EasyLanguage doesn't give us a reserved word or a function to help us keep track of pyramid entries, it does gives us the tools to come up with a solution. That solution comes to us by way of the keyword **currentShares** or **currentContracts**. Like **totalTrades** we can store the prior value in a variable and then compare the current value to determine the change in shares or contracts. So if the prior **currentShares** was equal to zero and the current **currentShares** is equal to two, then we know that two entries occurred. Since **currentShares** doesn't care if we are long or short, it is up to use to keep track of this.

```
if mp[1] <> 1 and mp = 1 then
    buysToday = buysToday + currentShares;
if mp[1] = mp and mp = 1 and currentShares > curShares then
    buysToday = buysToday + currentShares - curShares;
```

If **marketPosition** changes from **mp <> 1 to mp = 1** then we know an execution has taken place. Here **buysToday** is not incremented by one, but incremented by **currentShares**. We do this becase you can have multiple entries on a single bar. Since we are pyramiding, market position will stay constant after adding another position on so if market position is the same as it was on the prior bar, but currentShares has increased, then we know another execution has occurred. Finally, if you want to know the number of entries without worrying about the number of shares, you simply divide by **numSharesCons** (a user input value). Lets say you are trading 100 shares of Apple and you initiate a position, and then add on twice more your total position now stands at 300 shares. **BuysToday** is in terms of **curren-Shares** so **buysToday** would be equal to 300. Two of the inputs to this framework are **maxLongEntries** and **maxShortEntries**. If you don't want these values to be in terms of **numSharesCons** then you simply divide by **numSharesCons**. So the 300 shares of Apple becomes 3 long entries and not 300. This keeps the user from having to compute the **maxLongEntries** and **max-ShortEntries** in terms of what is considered an entry. That is if **numSharesCons** is greater than 1.

Here is how you incorporate this calculation into the buy directives. The same goes for the sell short directives.

```
if inStr(thePath,buyRevLev1Str) = 0 and l > buyRevLev1 and buysToday/numSharesCons < max-
LongEntries then
    buy("SLevABuy") numSharesCons shares next bar at buyRevLev1 limit;
if inStr(thePath,buyRevLev2Str) = 0 and l > buyRevLev2 and buysToday/numSharesCons < max-
LongEntries then
    buy("SLevBBuy") numSharesCons shares next bar at buyRevLev2 limit;
if inStr(thePath,buyRevLev3Str) = 0 and l > buyRevLev3 and buysToday/numSharesCons < max-
LongEntries then
    buy("SLevCBuy") numSharesCons shares next bar at buyRevLev3 limit;
```

One thing I discovered while using the framework was when I limited the maximum number of buys during the day to *two*, I often ended up with *three* buys. One more than I intended. Take a look at the following chart and you will see why.

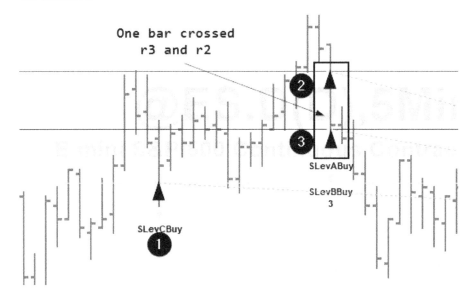

If you have more than two trade directives coded and since more than one entry can take place on a single bar, you can't completely control the max number of entries at the coding level. However, you can control it from the **Properties for All** dialog - *allow up to 2 entry orders in the same direction...* I did this and it indeed did work in the sense the number of entries were limited, however the performance deteriorated considerably.

Enumerating Path And Price Levels

The path keeps track of where the market has been and is used to constrain trade entries to only different Camarilla levels. You can enter a long position once at each r1, r2 and r3 and inversely only short positions at s1, s2 and s3. You can't duplicate entries at the same level. This marriage between the path of the market and order placement is very important. However, you want the user of the framework to be able to easily select different support and resistance levels to initiate and later on pyramid positions. There are two factors at work here, the history of the path and entry levels. So, to enable the user to select different support and resistance levels for trade execution, we will need to enumerate two variables. The code might explain this better.

```
if buyRevLevels = 1 then
begin
    buyRevLev1Str = "-s2";
    buyRevLev1 = s2;
    buyRevLev2Str = "-s3";
    buyRevLev2 = s3;
    buyRevLev3Str = "-s4";
    buyRevLev3 = s4;
end;
if buyRevLevels = 2 then
begin
    buyRevLev1Str = "-s1";
    buyRevLev1 = s1;
    buyRevLev2Str = "-s2";
    buyRevLev2 = s2;
    buyRevLev3Str = "-s3";
    buyRevLev3 = s3;
end;
if buyRevLevels <> 1 and buyRevLevels <> 2 then
begin
    buyRevLev1Str = "zzz";
    buyRevLev1 = s1;
    buyRevLev2Str = "zzz";
    buyRevLev2 = s2;
    buyRevLev3Str = "zzz";
    buyRevLev3 = s3;
end;
```

Similar to the algorithm from Tutorial 18, the user can iterate up to two different **buyRevLevels**. Each **buyRevLevel** describes the path location as a string **("-s2")** and the entry level as a price, **s2**. The string value is assigned to the variable **buyRevLev1Str** and the entry level is assigned to **buyRevLev1**. If the user steps out of bounds and uses a **buyRevLevels** that is not one or two, then a exception handler is used and assigns "zzz" to **buyRevLev1Str**. Here are the buy trade directives incorporated into the framework. First notice how I test for the exception "zzz"?

```
if time < lastEntryTime and waitBar > 3 and canTrade then
begin
  if buyRevLev1Str <> "zzz" then
  begin
   if inStr(thePath,buyRevLev1Str) = 0 and l > buyRevLev1 and
   buysToday < maxLongEntries then
      buy("SLevABuy") numSharesCons shares next bar at
```

```
      buyRevLev1 limit;
  if inStr(thePath,buyRevLev2Str) = 0 and l > buyRevLev2 and
  buysToday < maxLongEntries then
      buy("SLevBBuy") numSharesCons shares next bar at
          buyRevLev2 limit;
  if inStr(thePath,buyRevLev3Str) = 0 and l > buyRevLev3 and
  buysToday < maxLongEntries then
      buy("SLevCBuy") numSharesCons shares next bar at
          buyRevLev3 limit;
  end;
```

All the key components are now defined by the user via the inputs interface. Here is the code for enumerating the different options for **shortRevLevels1**.

```
//enumerate the universe of different Long Reversals
if shortRevLevels = 1 then
begin
    shortRevLev1Str = "+r2";
    shortRevLev1 = r2;
    shortRevLev2Str = "+r3";
    shortRevLev2 = r3;
    shortRevLev3Str = "+r4";
    shortRevLev3 = r4;
end;
if shortRevLevels = 2 then
begin
    shortRevLev1Str = "+r1";
    shortRevLev1 = r1;
    shortRevLev2Str = "+r2";
    shortRevLev2 = r2;
    shortRevLev3Str = "+r3";
    shortRevLev3 = r3;
end;
if shortRevLevels <> 1 and shortRevLevels <> 2 then
begin
    shortRevLev1Str = "zzz";
    shortRevLev1 = r1;
    shortRevLev2Str = "zzz";
    shortRevLev2 = r2;
    shortRevLev3Str = "zzz";
    shortRevLev3 = r3;
end;
```

Tradestation's Trade Listing Looks A Little Funny When Pyramiding

TradeStation reports each trade on a seperate line. So if you have a trade that pyramids for a total of two entries and gets stopped out this is what the trade listing report looks like.

```
3/29/2018 10:00    RLevBShort    $2,572.50    $0.00              1
3/29/2018 11:05    Stop Loss     $2,594.00                ($1,075.00)
3/29/2018 10:25    RLevCShort    $2,576.25    $0.00              1
3/29/2018 11:05    Stop Loss     $2,594.00                 ($887.50)
```

Here the **RLevBShort** position was put on at 10:00 and the market continue to rally so another short position was added at 10:25 at a better price (**RLevCShort**) and eventually the whole position was stopped out with $1,962.50 loss. This can seem a little confusing - it looks like the two trades are somewhat unrelated. I think it would be better to show the trades like this:

```
3/29/2018 10:00   RLevBShort  $2572.50
3/29/2018 10:25   RLevCShort  $2576.25
3/29/2018 11:05   Stop Loss   $2594.00    ($1.962.50)
```

Entryprice And Avg Entry Price

This framework also includes a trailing stop option that we first introduced in Tutorial 19. If you are pyramiding, the logic to exit on a trailing basis presented needs to be modified just a little bit. The problem is with how TradeStation only shows the first entry price in the **entryPrice** keyword. However TradeStation does offer the **avgEntryPrice** keyword/function which takes the total number of open positions and takes an average of the entry levels.

Assume you enter three positions the **ES** at 4700.75, 4698.50 and 4697.25, the avgEntryPrice would be (4700.75 + 4698.50 + 4697.25) / 3 or 4698.83. From there you can calculate the trailing stop similarly like we did in the previous tutorial. However, here you use **avgEntryPrice** in place of **entryPrice**.

```
if maxPositionProfit > trailPercentThresh$ then
    sell("LongTrail") next bar at avgEntryPrice +
    (1-trailPercent)*maxPositionProfit/bigPointValue/
    currentShares stop;
if maxPositionProfit > trailPercentThresh$ then
    buyToCover("ShortTrail") next bar at avgEntryPrice -
```

```
(1 - trailPercent) * maxPositionProfit/bigPointValue/
currentShares stop;
```

Once the profit threshold has been penetrated, the maximum position profit per share in terms of points multiplied by **(1 - trailPercent)** is used to either add to (for longs) or subtract from (for shorts) the **avgEntryPrice**. These levels will trail the price until new highs or new lows stop occurring. Eventually price will pull back or rise and the sell or buy stop is elected. The same logic to exit on a profit objective and a stop loss is the same as the other frameworks. Here are the best results after optimizing/iterating the framework.

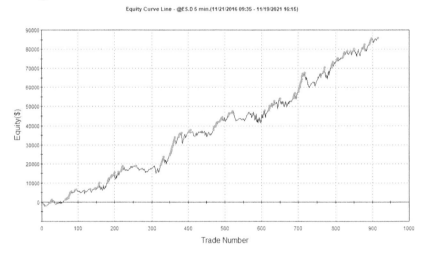

Equity Curve Line - @ES.D 5 min.(11/21/2016 09:35 - 11/19/2021 16:15)

TradeStation Performance Summary			Expand ⌄
	All Trades	**Long Trades**	**Short Trades**
Total Net Profit	$86,187.50	$43,825.00	$42,362.50
Gross Profit	$294,362.50	$149,912.50	$144,450.00
Gross Loss	($208,175.00)	($106,087.50)	($102,087.50)
Profit Factor	1.41	1.41	1.41
Total Number of Trades	913	460	453
Percent Profitable	63.96%	65.22%	62.69%
Winning Trades	584	300	284
Losing Trades	321	156	165
Even Trades	8	4	4
Avg. Trade Net Profit	$94.40	$95.27	$93.52
Avg. Winning Trade	$504.05	$499.71	$508.63
Avg. Losing Trade	($648.52)	($680.05)	($618.71)
Ratio Avg. Win:Avg. Loss	0.78	0.73	0.82
Largest Winning Trade	$1,450.00	$1,450.00	$1,450.00
Largest Losing Trade	($1,950.00)	($1,950.00)	($1,950.00)

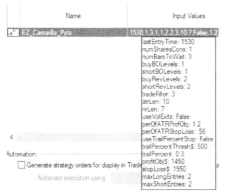

Here are the inputs to the framework. You can play around with it too, but it seems to like **buyRevLevels** and **shortRevLevels** set to **2**, a larger stop loss than profit objective, range expansion (**tradeFilter = 3**) and to disable **usePercenTrailingStop**. The performance looks decent; I really like the symmetry of the performance between long entries and short entries. This strategy is somewhat trend independent. I did a similar analysis on trading 500 shares of Apple and here are the performance metrics over the past five years.

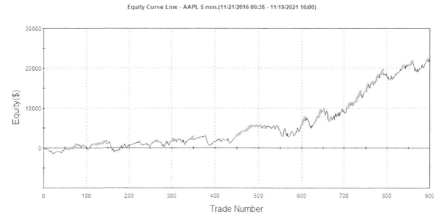

Summary Of Tutorial 20

This tutorial was quite lengthy due to the amount of new territory we covered. Pyramiding can be very powerful and very dangerous, so having a good grasp on how to program your scheme accurately is extremely important.

The Camarilla support and resistance levels were used as a foundation to build a multiple pyramiding algorithm. One where only counter-trend trades implemented via **limit** orders were allowed.

The limitations of **limit** orders were discussed and demonstrated through tests where order execution was allowed if the the limit price was touched and one where the market was forced to penetrate the limit price. The difference between the two techniques was dramatic.

Functionality of rounding up or down to the nearest tick was presented along with the associated EasyLanguage code. When dealing with limit orders, it is important to transform calculated price levels into accurate price levels denominated in the **minMove**.

Using string manipulation and concatenation was used to help record the market movement through the trading day. A string variable can act like a stack. A stack is a simple data structure where you can push information down in a single variable and pop off or search for the information you need. Once the strings for each individual level crossings are pushed down, they can be reviewed and acted on. The **inStr** built-in function was used to to search the **thePath** string. String variables can be used to simulate more advanced data structures.

Counting the number of buy and short entries when pyramiding can be be difficult. Code was presented that used the keywords **currentShares** or **currentContracts** to help accurately count long/short entries even when multiple entries occur on a single bar.

Enumeration was used again to allow TradeStation's optimization engine to iterate across different values and consequently over different blocks of logic.

The trailing stop mechanism that we programmed in an earlier tutorial, that depended on **entryPrice**, had to be reprogrammed to use **averageEntryPrice**.

The links to the **Tutorial 20** videos are:
Watch Me First!
https://vimeo.com/655371775/b9378b9cea

https://vimeo.com/655115350/d9151bf1ab

Strategies discussed in this Tutorial are:
EZ_Camarilla_Pyra

Indicators discussed in this Tutorial are:
CamarillaUseData2

TUTORIAL 21 -
PROGRAMMING A SCALE
OUT SCHEME

PUT TWO ON - TAKE A PROFIT ON FIRST AND PULL STOP TO BREAK-EVEN ON SECOND

T his tutorial will show you how to put two units on and after a specified profit has been reached, take the profit on the first unit and move the stop to break even on the second unit. If the market continues in a favorable direction, then take profit on the second unit. I will present this concept with two trading schemes, swing trading and day trading.

Swing Trading

There are multiple ways to swing trade. This is a somewhat generic term as it basically refers to any algorithm that trades on a short or intermediate time horizon. Many swing trading system use pure technical analysis to determine entry and exit levels. The swing system we will be employing in this tutorial seeks divergence between the long term and the short term trends. Or in other words a mean reversion approach. **Data2** as a daily bar will be used to help simplify calculations. In addition, it requires a move off of the open (an open time that is provided by the user) to provide evidence that the market is moving in the direction of the longer term trend.

Long Entry: enter long two units when the close of yesterday is greater than the 100 day moving average of closes and the rate of change (close - close[10]) is less than zero and the market breaks up a percentage of ATR.

Short Entry: enter short two units when the close of yesterday is less than the 100 day moving average of closes and the rate of change (close - close[10]) is greater than zero and the market breaks down a percentage of ATR

Place Protective Stop: liquidate both units at pre-defined loss level via a stop order. This risk amount can be a fixed dollar amount or an amount derived by using volatility.

Peel 1 Unit: a limit order is used to liquidate one unit at a pre-defined profit level. This profit level can be a fixed dollar amount or an amount derived by using volatility.
Move Stop To Break Even After Taking Profit: if one unit has been peeled off then move the stop on the other unit to a break even point. This produces a free trade.
Take Profit on Second Unit: similarly to taking profit on the first unit, a different profit level can be placed via a limit order based on a dollar or volatility amount.

Examples Of Trades

This first chart shows how the algorithm takes a profit on the first unit and pulls the stop to break even on the second unit. Eventually the price retraces enough to get out of the second unit at the original entry price.

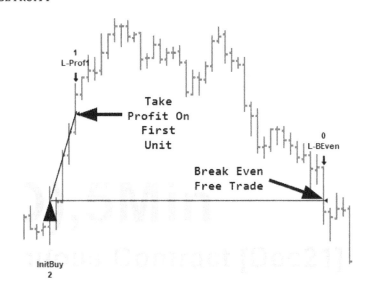

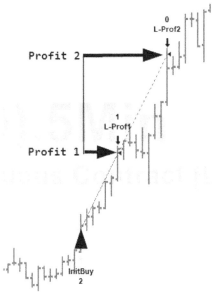

Here is an example of taking profits on both units. This example is what we, as traders, dream of. The market blasted off and hit the first profit rather quickly. At this point, one unit is peeled off and the stop for the second unit is brought up to break even. Initially after the first profit the market entered into a short congestion phase, but blasted off once again. The second profit was reached quickly and the secon unit was peeled off. This doesn't happen all that often.

Now this happens often. The break out was eventually the correct trade, however the risk parameter stopped the trade out for a loss. This is the ugly side of a stop loss, but it also has a beauti-

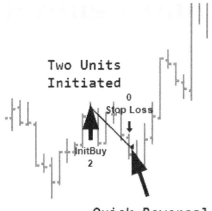

Two Units
Initiated

Quick Reversal
Both Units Out
With a Loss

ful side when the trade is completely wrong. Using two units in the @ES can be very risky, so it is probably best to err on the side of caution. So you have three exits in motion continuously: the double whammy stop out, the take profit on one and pull stop to break even, and take profit on both units. This algorithm is in the form of a framework as well. Take a look at these inputs.

TradeStation Strategies Applied	
EZ_Put2OnPeel1Off_BE_Swing(On)	

TradeStation Strategy Inputs	
Description	**Value**
EZ_Put2OnPeel1Off_BE_Swing - startTradeTime	700
EZ_Put2OnPeel1Off_BE_Swing - startTradeTimeOffSet	60
EZ_Put2OnPeel1Off_BE_Swing - endTradeTime	2100
EZ_Put2OnPeel1Off_BE_Swing - endTradeTimeOffSet	5
EZ_Put2OnPeel1Off_BE_Swing - numSharesCons	2
EZ_Put2OnPeel1Off_BE_Swing - scaleOutAmt	1
EZ_Put2OnPeel1Off_BE_Swing - movAvgLen	100
EZ_Put2OnPeel1Off_BE_Swing - momentumLen	9
EZ_Put2OnPeel1Off_BE_Swing - offsetPer1	0.24
EZ_Put2OnPeel1Off_BE_Swing - profitObj1$	650
EZ_Put2OnPeel1Off_BE_Swing - profitObj2$	1500
EZ_Put2OnPeel1Off_BE_Swing - stopLoss$	550
EZ_Put2OnPeel1Off_BE_Swing - useVolExits	False
EZ_Put2OnPeel1Off_BE_Swing - perOfATRProfObj1	2.05
EZ_Put2OnPeel1Off_BE_Swing - perOfAtrProfObj2	3
EZ_Put2OnPeel1Off_BE_Swing - perOfATRStopLoss	1.05
EZ_Put2OnPeel1Off_BE_Swing - tradeFilter	0
EZ_Put2OnPeel1Off_BE_Swing - atrLen	10
EZ_Put2OnPeel1Off_BE_Swing - atrMult	1
EZ_Put2OnPeel1Off_BE_Swing - nrLen	7

This framework is very similar to the others that have been presented thus far. Here is the new inputs and a review of some that have already been presented.

startTradeTime and **startTradeTimeOffSet** - this value allows the user to define the open time to use for the range break out. If you want to use the open of the 7:00 a.m. bar, then you set this value to 700 and the **startTradeTimeOffSet** to 5. If you want to optimize a delay from this benchmark time, then you can optimize the **startTradeTimeOffSet** in increments of the **barInterval**. If you want to use a time prior to this benchmark, then you would optimize in negative increments of the **barInterval**.

endTradeTime and **endTradeTimeOffSet** - this value allows the user to define the time to stop allowing entry orders. If you want to allow users up to the 9:00 p.m. bar, then you set this value to 2100 and the **endTradeTimeOffSet** to 5. If you want to optimize a delay from this benchmark time, then you can optimize the **endTradeTimeOffSet** in increments of the **barInterval**. If you want to use a time prior to this benchmark, then you would optimize in negative increments of the **barInterval**.

scaleOutAmt - this value is connected to **numSharesCons** and tells TradeStation to carve out this value at the first profit objective. This value should be less than **numSharesCons**.

movAvgLen - this value determines the direction of the longer term trend
$$\text{average(close of data2,movAvgLen)}$$

MomentumLen - determines the look back to capture the short term rate of change.
$$\text{(close[0] of data2- close[momentumLen] of data2)}$$

OffSetPer1 - the percentage amount of the ATR to determine the break out for longs and shorts.

ProfitObj1$ - the dollar value of the profit objective for the first unit. If this is set to $750, then a profit is taken at $750.

ProfitObj2$ - the dollar value of the profit objective for the second unit in total. If this value is set to $1,800, then once $1,800 is reached with the remaining number of units it is is taken.

StopLoss$ - the total amount to risk for the total number of units.

UseVolExits - instead of using fixed dollar amounts, the user can determine percentages or multiples of the ATR for total risk, profit1 and profit2.

PerOfAtrProfObj1 - percentage of ATR to take profit on the first unit.

PerOfAtrProfObj2 - percentage of ATR to take profit on the second unit.

PerOfAtrStopLoss - percentage of ATR to risk on initial trade - full complement of units.

This framework can optimize millions of combinations of the inputs. Here is the equity curve without trade execution costs on the 24 hour @ES futures contract when using volatility based risk and reward inputs. If you want to maximize the equity curve, this seemed the way to go. However, the draw down metric was quite high. Risking 0.25 of 10-Day ATR (can get quite large), taking profits on 1st unit at 1.75 ATR and then profits at 2.75 ATR produced over $115K with a maximum intraday draw down of over $35K. Remember the break even stop is invoked once the first unit is taken off the table at a profit. The average trade was relatively large at $615. The trend filter (100-Day Moving Average) eliminated many short trades so there was definitely asymmetry. Trade entry was limited between 8:00 a.m. and 9:00 p.m. Exits were not time constrained.

Equity Curve Line - @ES 5 min.(10/31/2016 18:05 - 12/10/2021 17:00)

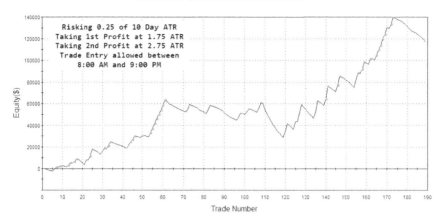

Risking 0.25 of 10 Day ATR
Taking 1st Profit at 1.75 ATR
Taking 2nd Profit at 2.75 ATR
Trade Entry allowed between
8:00 AM and 9:00 PM

Equity Curve Line - @ES 5 min.(10/31/2016 18:05 - 12/10/2021 17:00)

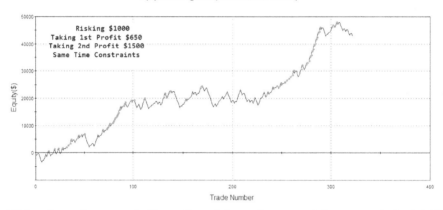

Risking $1000
Taking 1st Profit $650
Taking 2nd Profit $1500
Same Time Constraints

This chart is uses dollars for risk and reward inputs. Sub $10K drawdown.

Now The Code

There are two windows based on time used in this algorithm. The first window encapsulates the entire trading session and gathers the necessary calculations to execute the trades such as the longer term moving average, shorter term rate of change and the ATR calculation. The second window size is controlled by the user via the inputs. This user defined window specifies the time boundaries for new entries.

Here is the first window where the majority of calculations occur; it opens on the first bar of the new session. The first thing you will notice is a **DOW** analysis.

```
startTime = sessionStartTime(0,1);
endTime   = sessionEndtime(0,1);


endTimeOffSet = 0;
if t = calcTime(startTime,barInterval) then
begin
   if totalTrades > totDailyTrades then //DOW ANALYSIS START
   begin
     switchValue = iff(currentShares = 0,entryDate(1),entryDate);
     switch(dayOfWeek(switchValue)
     begin
        Case 1: MProf = MProf + (netProfit - begDayEquity);
        Case 2: TProf = TProf + (netProfit - begDayEquity);
        Case 3: WProf = WProf + (netProfit - begDayEquity);
        Case 4: RProf = RProf + (netProfit - begDayEquity);
        Case 5: FProf = FProf + (netProfit - begDayEquity);
        Default: Value1 = Value1 + 1;
     end;
     begDayEquity = netProfit;
     totDailyTrades = totalTrades;
   end;
   ATRValue = avgTrueRange(atrLen) of data2;
   ATRMin = lowest(truerange of data2,nrLen);
   trendFilter = iff(close of data2>average(c of data2,100),1,-1);
      momFilter =
     iff(close of data2 -close[momentumLen] of data2 > 0,1,-1);

   if tradeFilter = 0 then canTrade = True;

   if tradeFilter = 1 then
   begin
      canTrade = truerange of data2 < ATRValue;
   end;
   if tradeFilter = 2 then
   begin
      canTrade = trueRange of data2 = ATRMin;
   end;
   if tradeFilter = 3 then
   begin
      canTrade = trueRange of data2 > ATRValue;
   end;
end;
```

This DOW analysis is a little different than the one presented earlier. The reason for this is this algorithm is not a day trader. This code, when triggered, will find the original entry date of the trade, which can span multiple days, and attribute the trade profit/loss to that day of week. If a new trade is entered on a Monday and the first scale out doesn't occur until Wednesday, then the profit or loss generated by that trade is be put into the Monday accumulator. You will notice a new function call.

```
switchValue = iff(currentShares = 0,entryDate(1),entryDate);
```

The **IFF** function was developed by TradeStation and is very useful as it cuts down on coding and is pretty self explanatory. This function returns the first value, in this case - **entryDate(1)**, if the condition, **currentShares = 0** is **True**, else the second value **entryDate** is returned. Here is the code the IFF replicates.

```
if(currentShares = 0) then
    returnVal = entryDate(1)
else
    returnVal = entryDate;
```

You will find that I use the **IFF** function a few times in this algorithm. I like it because it works, cuts down on extra lines of code, and is self explanatory. The **entryDate** of trade depends on if the prior trade was completely or partially liquidated. If a trade was completely closed out, then the entry date of the trade is referenced by passing a 1 to the function-like keyword **entry-Date(1)**. If only a portion of the trade's position was liquidated, then the trade is still open and you refer to its entry date by simply examining **entryDate** with out a parameter or with a zero value **entryDate(0)**. Many of the EasyLanguage built-in arrays, keywords, or functions truncate the parameter list or index if it is **zero**.

```
high = high[0];
entryDate = entryDate(0);
entryPrice = entryPrice(0);
```

So the **switchValue** depends on if the prior trade was completely or partially liquidated. The rest of the code in this window does all the necessary calculations to determine if a trade occurs and the base values to determine entry price (**Data2** is ued for these calcuations.)

The next window defines the time span where new trades are allowed to be entered. When trading the 24 hour market there may be times when you don't want to enter a new position. Entering trades at 2:00 a.m. may not be your cup of tea, but having a market open for nearly 24 hours to exit might be. In managing funds, we would use this hybrid entry/exit methodology to trade our algorithms. Many times exiting a trade in the middle of the night on a low volume "knee jerk" was costly. However, having the ability to execute instead of waiting provided a certain level of security. Was the price of this security worth it? In the long run maybe, but it did provide a client some peace of mind. For this reason, I have imparted this capability into the framework.

```
if t = calcTime(startTradeTime,startTradeTimeOffSet) then
begin
    openTick = open;
    myBarCount = 0;
    buysToday = 0;
    shortsToday = 0;
    stb = roundToNearestTick(openTick+offSetPer1*ATRValue,"Up");
    sts = roundToNearestTick(openTick-offSetPer1*ATRValue,"Down");
    loss$ = stopLoss$;
    profit1$ = profitObj1$;
    profit2$ = profitObj2$;
    if useVolExits then
    begin
        loss$ = perOfATRStopLoss * ATRValue *
            bigPointValue * numSharesCons;
        profit1$ = perOfATRProfObj1 * ATRValue *
            bigPointValue * (numSharesCons - scaleOutAmt) ;
        profit2$ = perOfATRProfObj2 * ATRValue *
            bigPointValue* scaleOutAmt;
    end;
end;
```

If the **startTradeTime+startTradeTimeOffset** is encountered, then the **openTick** is collected and the break out values, **stb** and

sts, are calculated and rounded to the nearest tick. Here you are using the data that closed at 5:00 p.m. or 1700 the prior day to do your calculations. Basically you are ignoring the market action from 1700 to 700 for order placement. And you are carving out a slice of the day to allow entry orders.

```
if  t-endTimeoffSet < calcTime(endTradeTime,endTradeTimeOffSet) then
begin
    if trendFilter = 1 and momFilter = -1 and canTrade and
    currentShares = 0 and buysToday = 0 then
        buy("InitBuy") numSharesCons shares next bar at stb stop;

    if trendFilter = -1 and momFilter = 1 and canTrade and
    currentShares = 0 and shortsToday= 0 then
        sellShort("InitShort") numSharesCons shares next bar at
            sts stop;
end;
```

Here you can only enter a trade between **startTradeTime** and **endTradeTime**. In addition, you can only go long when the **trendFilter** equals one and **momFilter** equals negative one, divergence. Flip the **trendFilter** and **momFilter** to enter a short position.

The trade management code runs around the clock. This is where all of the magic takes place. Review the code and the highlighted areas. See if it makes sense. After the code I will go through it.

```
if mp = 1 then
begin
if currentShares = numSharesCons then
    sell("L-Prof1") scaleOutAmt shares next bar at
        roundToNearestTick(entryPrice+profit1$/bigPointValue,"Dn")
            limit;
    if currentShares = numSharesCons - scaleOutAmt then
    begin
      sell("L-BEven") next bar entryPrice stop;
      sell("L-Prof2") next bar at
        roundToNearestTick(entryPrice+profit2$/bigPointValue,"Dn")
            limit;
    end;
end;
if mp = -1 then
begin
```

```
if currentShares = numSharesCons then
  buyToCover("S-Prof1") scaleOutAmt shares next bar at
    roundToNearestTick(entryPrice-profit1$/bigPointValue,"Up")
      limit;
  if currentShares = numSharesCons - scaleOutAmt then
  begin
    buyToCover("S-BEven") next bar entryPrice stop;
    buyToCover("S-Prof2") next bar at
      roundToNearestTick(entryPrice+profit2$/bigPointValue,"Up")
      limit;
  end;
end;

totTrades = totalTrades;
curShares = currentShares;
SetStopPosition;
setStopLoss(loss$);
```

If a long position is on (**mp** = 1), the first thing that is examined is the number of contracts/shares that are currently in the market. If **currentShares** equals **numSharesCons**, then the full allocation is in play via the initial trade. The computer is then looking to unload **scaleOutAmt** shares at a profit (**profit1$**), or the entire position at a loss, **loss$**. Remember **profit1$**, **profit2$** and **loss$** were calculated based on either a pre-defined dollar or volatility amount. When the first profit is taken at **profit1$**, then **currentShares** becomes [**numSharesCons - scaleOutAmt**], because the **scaleOutAmt** shares are liquidated. Notice how we had to specify the amount amount of **shares** to peel off. Now, since a profit has been taken on the first lot, you will either unload the remaining shares at our original **entryPrice** on a stop or at **profit2$** on a limit. The second amount of shares has become a "Free Trade"; one that will not theoretically lose money if you exclude execution costs. You could always add/subtract a tick or two from the **entryPrice** to cover these costs. Keeping track of the **totalTrades** and **curShares** in bar array variables allows us to compare previous bar values to current values. This helps us determine if the **currentShares** or **totalTrades** have changed and if so take the proper actions. This last bit of code simply prints out the DOW analysis on a specific date at a specifi time.

```
if d = 1211124 and t = 1100 then
begin
    print(d," DOW Analysis ");
    print("Monday    : ",MProf);
    print("Tuesday   : ",TProf);
    print("Wednesday : ",WProf);
    print("Thursday  : ",RProf);
    print("Friday    : ",FProf);

end;
```

Convert Framework To A Day Trader

The conversion of this existing code to make it a daytrading framework is quite easy.

1.) Collect open tick on the first bar of the day session.

```
if t = calcTime(startTime,barInterval) then
begin
   openTick = open;
```

2.) Since we don't need to worry about the midnight 0000 time stamp, we need to modify the trading window. Here we will need to test the **startTradeTime** and take the minimum between the **sessionEndTime** and the users **endTradeTime**. This will ensure trades are issued during the correct time periods.

```
if t>=calcTime(startTradeTime,startTradeTimeOffSet) and t <
minList(calcTime(endTradeTime,endTradeTimeOffSet),endTime) then
```

3.) Add **setExitOnClose** functionality.

```
setExitOnClose;
```

That is it. You will have both versions in the ELD that you can download from the website.

$$\triangle\triangle\triangle$$

Summary Of Tutorial 21

This algorithm could be labeled **Put N On - Take N/2 At Profit - Pull Break Even on N/2 Or Take Another N/2 Profit**. This sounds intriguing because you potentially get a free trade. If you are fortunate to get a profit on the first N/2, then the remaining N/2, worst case, gets out at a break even, and best case with another profit. However, don't let this idea hide the fact you could get stopped out with a full compliment of N. Nothing feels worse than putting on more than one unit and getting stopped out without a chance to take a profit. This is a very popular algorithm for day traders.

This algorithm isn't limited to day trading though and a swing trading version was presented. The swing version allows the user to carve out a trading section of the 24 hour market. This allows the user to enter trades during higher volume periods and provides a level of security in the ability to get out at anytime - no waiting.

If you need to extract the **entryPrice** for accounting purposes (like or DOW Analysis), then you need to know if you have either fully liquidated or just partially. Full liquidation allows you to index into the **entryPrice**(1) function by passing it a 1. Partial liquidations necessitates passing either a 0 to **entryPrice(0)** or simply using the name **entryPrice**.

You can apply different trade directives by examining the **currentShares** that are currently held.

```
If currentShares = 200 then
    sell next bar at...
If currentShares = 100 then
    sell next bar at...
```

The highly useful **IFF** function was introduced. Remember if the Boolean comparison is True, then the first expression is executed and its results are passed back the variable via assignment. If the Boolean test fails, then the results of the second expression are passed back.

```
aVal = 2
xVal = IFF(aVal = 2, aVal - 2, aVal+1)
xVal = 0

aVal = 4
xVal = IFF(aVal = 2, aVal - 2, aVal+1)
xVal = 5
```

The link to the **Tutorial 21** video is:
https://vimeo.com/659396251/fcbed00c8f

Strategies discussed in this Tutorial are:
EZ_Put2OnPeelOff_BE_Day

TUTORIAL 22- CRAWLING LIKE A BUG ON A FIVE MINUTE CHART

MAKE TRADING DECISIONS BASED ON INTRADAY MARKET ACTIVITY OR HOW A LITTLE WORM BECOMES A BEAUTIFUL BUTTERFLY

Imagine you are a small worm and you squirm along the path of the five minute bars as they reveal themselves. With this Tutorial you will be able to follow this worm along its journey and monitor it as it transforms first into a bug and then into a butterfly. Once the worm is transformed into a butterfly it then can either take flight or disappear. Once in flight its destination is determined by the trade management module. PASSWORD: **Turing**.

At this point in the Tutorial you will probably stop reading and Google to see if North Carolina allows recreational use of marijuana or acid - one of the two - probably learning toward acid. You will find out it allows **neither**.

The algorithm that is presented, through the life cycle of worm, bug, butterfly could be labeled "Bounce", "BackFire" or "Flinch", because we are going to buy on pullbacks and sell short on rallies after certain patterns present themselves. The pattern recognition will be handled by a **Finite State Machine**. As you may know computer science borrows much from biology. Artificial Intelligence is a manifestation of computer computation and two of its components, **Genetic Optimization** and **Artificial Neural Networks**. These concepts are deeply rooted in evolution and brain modeling respectively. Describing the FSM in terms of a worm's life cycle, might provide more insight than using normal numerical syntax. In this analogy, we are going to allow the user to specify the duration when our little worm starts and ends its journey, and the conditions where it transforms to a little bug and then into butterfly. The transformations are simply state transitions. The transformation to butterfly must take place during the day session or it starts over.

Long Entry:
The little worm traces its way along the five minute bar path keeping track of its peaks sand its valleys. This little worm is smart, because it can remember the highest peak and its associated time and the deepest valley and its time during the course of its journey. Once the little worm moves X% of ATR(N) from its *highest peak* it transforms into a little bug.

The little bug continues this journey along the 5-minute bar path. It is equipped with an RSI monitor and after the RSI monitor crosses above the **OverSold** zone, the little bug checks the next bar to make sure it is still located below the deepest valley stored by the little worm (its prior state) - it has quite a good memory. If the RSI and the little bug's location aligns, then the little bug transforms into a butterfly.

This little butterfly will either fly or disappear at the end of the **butterflyLife**. Its survival depends on two conditions: 1) the current **RSI(Close,Y)** is still above the **OverSold** zone and 2) the following bar rises above the **highest high of the past two bars**. If it survives it takes flight by taking a **long** position. The life cycle ends if either of the two conditions are not met within a certain amount of time.

Short Entry:
Just like the long entry the little worm traces its way along the five minute bar path keeping track of its peaks and its valleys all the while keeping track of the highest and deepest peaks/valleys and their associated time stamps. Once the little worm moves X % of ATR(N) from its *deepest valley* it transforms into a little bug.

The little bug continues this journey along the five minute bar path. As you know it is equipped with a RSI monitor and once the RSI monitor crosses above **RSI(close**, Y), the little bug makes sure it is located above the highest peak stored by the little worm (its prior state) - it has quite a good memory. If the RSI and the little bug's location aligns, then the little bug transforms into a beautiful butterfly.

Just like the long entry, this little butterfly will either fly or disappear. Its survival depends on two conditions: 1) the current **RSI(Close,Y)** is still above the **OverBought** zone and 2) the following bar drops below the **lowest low of the past two bars** within the time span of the **butterflyLife** . If it survives it takes flight by taking a short position. The life cycle ends if either of the two condition are not met.

From there the little butterfly's journey will end either by finding a home in a well kept flower bed or be smashed against the window of an oncoming vehicle. These two eventualities will be determined by our trade management module, a nice profit or a loss. *Note: no actual animals were harmed in this highly descriptive analog.*

Since the little worm changes states we will use a simple **Finite State Machine** (FSM) and the associated **switch-case** construct, to determine if the worm transforms into either a **bull** or **bear**

bug/butterfly. Here are the guts of the FSM - see if it makes a little bit of sense to you.

```
switch (lilBug)
begin
    // always start out as a worm
    case("worm"):
        if h > lilBugPeak then
                begin
            lilBugPeak = high;
            lilBugPeakTime = t;
        end;
        if l < lilBugValley then
        begin
            lilBugValley = low;
            lilBugValleyTime = t;
        end;
                    //can the worm transform to bull or bear bug
        if lilBugPeak-lilBugValley>bugDropRisePer*ATRValue then
        begin
            if lilBugValleyTime > lilBugPeakTime then
            begin
                lilBug = "bullBug";
            end;
            if lilBugValleyTime < lilBugPeakTime then
            begin
                lilBug = "bearBug";
            end;
        end;
//  bullBug transformation
    case("bullBug"):
        if rsi(c,rsiLen) crosses above bugOverSold and
        l < lilBugValley then
        begin
            lilBug = "bullButterfly";
        end;
    case("bullButterfly"):
        if time < calcTime(bugEndTime,bugEndTimeOffSet) and
        rsi(c,rsiLen) > bugOverSold then
            buy numSharesCons shares next bar at
                highest(h,numTrigBars) stop;
        value97 = value97 + 1;
        if value97 >= butterflyLife then
        begin
            lilBug = "";
            value97 = 0;
        end;
//  bearBug transformation
    case("bearBug"):
        if rsi(c,rsiLen) crosses below bugOverBot and
        h > lilBugPeak then
        begin
```

```
        lilBug = "bearButterfly";
    end;
    case("bearButterfly"):
    if time < calcTime(bugEndTime,bugEndTimeOffSet) and
    rsi(c,rsiLen) < bugOverBot then
        sellShort numSharesCons shares next bar at
            lowest(l,numTrigBars) stop;
    value96 = value96 + 1;
    if value96 >= butterflyLife then
    begin
        lilBug = "";
        value96 = 0;
    end;
end;
```

Using just one **FSM** requires us to use two different types of bugs, a **bullBug** and a **bearBug**. Once the worm has moved from a peak to a valley or a valley to a peak that equates to a distance of **bugDropRisePer X ATR**, then one comparison determines if it becomes of **bullBug** or a **bearBug** - the chronological order of the peak and the valley. If the valley occurs after the peak then we have a **bullBug**. Conversely, if the peak is made last, then we have a **bearBug**. The time stamps of these market extremes are stored in the **lilBugPeakTime** and **lilBugValleyTime** variables.

Once the **FSM** determines the class of bug, it branches to the correct state. If the **bullBug** crosses above the **overSold** zone and it is at or below the **worm's** deepest valley it transforms into a **bullButterfly**. To be 100% accurate, the bull or bear butterfly lives for **butterflyLife** (user input) bars. In EasyLanguage's implementation of the **switch-case**, once a state transitions it must re-enter the **switch-case** at the top for it to take effect. In other words, once a a **bullBug** transforms into a **bullButterfly**, it must wait one additional bar for the **bullButterfly** logic to be applied. Once the flow of the logic enters into the **bullButterfly** case, then it either lives or expires within a limited amount of time.

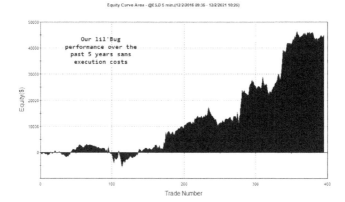

If the **bearBug** crosses below the **overBought** zone and it is at or above the **worm's** highest peek it transforms into a **bear-Butterfly**. The performance shown is sans execution costs (5-year record) on one contract of @ES.D. This algorithm is trend neutral, it doesn't care which direction the overall trend is headed. The number of long versus short entries is relatively symmetrical. However, the long side performance greatly underperforms the short side. The average trade is respectable at north of $100.

The code presented in encased into a framework. The user can modify many of the inputs such as the distance between the highest peak and the deepest valley, the number of days in the ATR and RSI calculation. The ove-bought and over-sold zone boundaries can also be changed. The trade management module allows dollars or volatility to determine exit. The window of where the little worm begins its journey and where the last trade entry is allowed can be modified by the user too!

```
if time = calcTime(bugStartTime,bugStartTimeOffSet) then
begin
    lilBug = "worm";
    lilBugPeak = h;
    lilBugPeakTime = t;
    lilBugValley = l;
    lilBugValleyTime = t;
end;
```

Time constraints are used in the **FSM** too.

```
case("bullButterfly"):
  if time < calcTime(bugEndTime,bugEndTimeOffSet) and
  rsi(c,rsiLen) > bugOverSold then
    buy numSharesCons shares next bar at highest(h,2) stop;
  lilBug = "";
```

The typical trade managment code is used in this framework.
```
SetStopPosition;
setStopLoss(loss$);
setProfitTarget(profit$);
setExitOnClose;
```

Convert Strategy Code To A Show Me To Help Determine Accurate Trade Entry

When I first programmed this technique years ago I did not model it with a **FSM**. I was surprised that the performance deteriorated when the butterfly was allowed to live more than two bars. So like I do on other programming projects I quickly converted the code to a **ShowMe**. I could have done the same with a **PaintBar**. In the **ShowMe** I wanted to highlight the bar where the worm transformed into a butterfly. All you need to do is take out any mention of a trade directive (**buy, sell, sellShort, cover**) and any references that deal with a market position. In place of the trade directives, simply put a Plot1 and/or Plot2. Here is the pertinet code of the **ShowMe**.

```
case("bullBug"):
  if rsi(c,rsiLen) crosses above bugOverSold and l<lilBugValley then
    lilBug = "bullButterfly";
case("bullButterfly"):
  if time < calcTime(bugEndTime,bugEndTimeOffSet) and
  rsi(c,rsiLen) > bugOverSold then
    plot1(High);
  lilBug = "";
case("bearBug"):
  if rsi(c,rsiLen) crosses below bugOverBot and h > lilBugPeak then
    lilBug = "bearButterfly";
case("bearButterfly"):
  if time < calcTime(bugEndTime,bugEndTimeOffSet) and
  rsi(c,rsiLen) < bugOverBot then
    plot2( Low);
  lilBug = "";
```

The **ShowMe** will show when the bug transforms into a

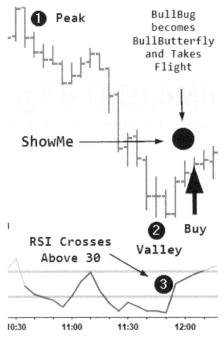

Peak ❶

BullBug becomes BullButterfly and Takes Flight

ShowMe ⟶

RSI Crosses Above 30

❷ Buy
Valley

❸

10:30   11:00   11:30   12:00

butterfly. You may or may not see a trade at a **ShowMe** bar because it didn't survive and did not take flight. Here is a chart demonstrating the Lil' Bug Strategy and ShowMe. In this example the Valley is made last, therefore the **worm** transforms into a **bullBug** and then into **bullButterfly**. This example shows the survival and flight of the bug. Follow along the chart and you can see the key chart patterns that initiates the long entry.

In this next example, the Peak is made last so we are dealing with a **BearBug**. The ShowMe demonstrates the transformation to butterfly, but unfortunately this little butterfly doesn't survive and doesn't take flight. The next bar did not penetrate the lowest low of the past two bars. This was probably for the best. In fact it was for the best because the market continued to rally into the close of the day. With the assist-

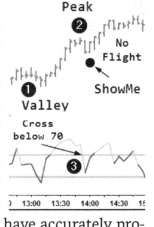

Peak
❷   No Flight
ShowMe
❶
Valley
Cross below 70
❸

13:00 13:30 14:00 14:30 15

ance of a **ShowMe** you can make sure you have accurately programmed your ideas.

Here the worm is placed on the chart near the 10:30 bar and starts it journey.

It hits the peak very quickly and then the valley within two bars. At this point it transforms into a bug. The bug quickly transforms into a butterfly on the crossing above the **overSold** boundary. The butterfly checks the RSI value (> 30) and then takes

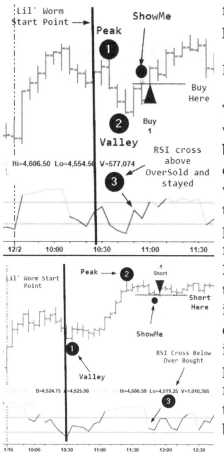

flight at the highest high of the past two bars.

Here is another example.

This chart demonstrates the lil' worm's transformation into a **bearBug**. Remember only one condition determines a bear versus a bull bug - the timing of the peaks and valleys. Here the peak was made last and therefore the worm became a **bear-Bug**. Once a **bearBug** it will only transform into a **bearButterfly** if the RSI crosses below the **overBought** boundary. Its ability to survive and take flight depends on the location of the RSI reading and the penetration of the lowest low of the past two bars.

What Should You Expect If You Increase Resolution

You should not expect to get the same results if you increase resolution to a one minute chart with the *"Bug Algorithm"*. There are are basic three reasons for this.

1) The reading of the RSI on a one minute chart is different than a five minute chart. One chart might dip into an extreme zone whereas the other does not. The five minute bar feeds the RSI calculation every five minutes and includes the highest high and lowest low of the past 5 one minute bars. The one minute chart feeds the RSI every minute and just has the high and the low of

the current bar.

2) The highest high or lowest low of the past 2 five minute bars is equivalent to the highest high or lowest low of the past 10 one minute bars.

3) The life of the butterfly is denominated in five minute bars. In our testing, the butterfly has five minutes to complete the entry criteria to take flight. If you test this on a one minute bar, then the life of the butterfly would have to be set to 5 one minute bars.

To enable you to test this I have included two more user inputs into the **ShowMe** and **Strategy**. You can now control the number of trigger bars to look back and the number of bars the butterly lives. Also you might want to play around with the RSI look back bars.

Here are the settings for the five minute bar chart.

TradeStation Strategy Inputs	
Description	Value
EZ_LilBug_Algorithm - bugStartTime	930
EZ_LilBug_Algorithm - bugStartTimeOffSet	60
EZ_LilBug_Algorithm - bugEndTime	1545
EZ_LilBug_Algorithm - bugEndTimeOffSet	-5
EZ_LilBug_Algorithm - bugDropRisePer	0.39
EZ_LilBug_Algorithm - rsiLen	3
EZ_LilBug_Algorithm - bugOverBot	70
EZ_LilBug_Algorithm - bugOverSold	30
EZ_LilBug_Algorithm - numTrigBars	2
EZ_LilBug_Algorithm - butterflyLife	1
EZ_LilBug_Algorithm - numSharesCons	1
EZ_LilBug_Algorithm - profitObj$	500
EZ_LilBug_Algorithm - stopLoss$	500
EZ_LilBug_Algorithm - useVolExits	True
EZ_LilBug_Algorithm - atrLen	10
EZ_LilBug_Algorithm - perOfATRProfObj	1.2
EZ_LilBug_Algorithm - perOfATRStopLoss	0.6

And here are the settings for the one minute bar chart.

TradeStation Strategy Inputs	
Description	**Value**
EZ_LilBug_Algorithm - bugStartTime	930
EZ_LilBug_Algorithm - bugStartTimeOffSet	60
EZ_LilBug_Algorithm - bugEndTime	1545
EZ_LilBug_Algorithm - bugEndTimeOffSet	-5
EZ_LilBug_Algorithm - bugDropRisePer	0.39
EZ_LilBug_Algorithm - rsiLen	4
EZ_LilBug_Algorithm - bugOverBot	70
EZ_LilBug_Algorithm - bugOverSold	30
EZ_LilBug_Algorithm - numTrigBars	5
EZ_LilBug_Algorithm - butterflyLife	1
EZ_LilBug_Algorithm - numSharesCons	1
EZ_LilBug_Algorithm - profitObj$	500
EZ_LilBug_Algorithm - stopLoss$	500
EZ_LilBug_Algorithm - useVolExits	True
EZ_LilBug_Algorithm - atrLen	10
EZ_LilBug_Algorithm - perOfATRProfObj	1.2
EZ_LilBug_Algorithm - perOfATRStopLoss	0.6

Even with the modifications to the parameters that seem to re-flect same time span between one and five minute bars, you will still get different results. That is why it is important to trade the time resolution that you used in the development of the algorithm.

△△△

Summary Of Tutorial 22

Sometimes using a simple analogy such as the life of a bug to explain a somewhat complicated computer process helps a reader understand the overall concept. Pattern recognition can be difficult. Understanding and programming chronological sequences that fit a certain criteria when reduced to a simple analogy can make all the difference in the world. Once you start using **FSMs** you will *not* go back to using flags (Boolean values that are turned off/on when certain conditions are met), extraneous variables and your programming productivity will increase considerably.

The most efficient and cleanest method to program a multiple step pattern is best handled by a **FSM**. The **swith-case** construct is the easiest way to implement a **FSM**.

A good way to confirm your programming accuracy is to convert your strategy to a **ShowMe**. In place of trade directives, you use **Plot** near the high and low of a bar that finalizes the last state of the **FSM**. If the **ShowMe** and the **Strategy** don't agree then you know you have a problem inside your code.

Pattern recognition is highly dependent on time frames. A five minute bar pattern will not produce the same results of the same pattern applied to a one minute bar. Trade what you test!

Pattern recognition is scaleable. Once you program the **FSM** for the pattern you can apply it to any time frame. However, the values and even the code that promotes the state transitions will need to be modified, in most cases. In rare cases, you can apply your **FSM** code to different resolutions without any modifications. These are algorithms that search for pure price movements and don't really rely on indicators.

The link to the **Tutorial 21** video is:
https://vimeo.com/659394166/509a300465

Strategies discussed in this Tutorial are:
EZ_LilBug_Algorithm

ShowMes discussed in this Tutorial are:
EZ_LilBug_ShowMe

Indicators discussed in this Tutorial are:
RSI

TUTORIAL 23 - TEMPLATES FOR FURTHER RESEARCH

W hat good is a book that teaches programming if you can't take what you have read and apply it to your current programming needs. Much of what I have discussed is a bunch of theories that have some simple algorithms associated with them. These simple algorithms are designed to show how the theory is applied. However, in many cases, the algorithms are not generic enough for a newer programmer to take and modify to fit their needs. The frameworks that I have shown and included in the supplemental material should work right out of the box with very little modifications. In most cases, you just need to fiddle with the inputs. In thisTutorial I am going to present some templates that are more generic and open to more customization than the ones I have disclosed through out the text. The complete codes that have been described will be included along with these templates. I promised in one of the earlier Tutorials a function that will pack daily arrays with daily (or user defined daily timeframes) data so that more than just one or two days of history can be referenced if a daily **data2** is not used.

Template1

EZ_Template1_5Min - this template is derived from Tutorials 14 and 15. All data is derived from the five minute bar. This template shows how to use the high of the prior day and the low of the prior day to determine entry levels. A max of two long and two short positions are allowed on a daily basis. In addition a stop loss and profit objective are used as well. When using just five minute bar data it is difficult to derive the number of days a position has been in effect. This template introduces a **DaysSinceEntryExit** exit technology. The user can specify the max number of days a position from a single entry can be maintained. After the the number of days a position has in effect reaches the user input, then the position is liquidated at the next session's open. Here are the snippets of code that provides this capability.

```
inputs:useSettlement(False),settlementTime(1600),
settlementFormula(1),daysSinceEntryExit(5),
stopLoss$(500),profitObj$(1000);
```

```
//first bar of the day
if t = StartTime + barInterval then
begin
    HighOfDay1 = 0;
    LowOfDay1  = 999999999;
    if mp <> 0 then daysSinceEntry = daysSinceEntry + 1;
end;
```

Reset **daysSinceEntry** to zero when the market position becomes flat or a position is closed out.

```
//reset daysSinceEntry to zero when..
if mp = 0 then daysSinceEntry = 0;
if priorBuysToday < buysToday or priorShortsToday < shortsToday then
        daysSinceEntry = 0;
```

When the **daysSinceEntry** reaches the specified number of days that equal the user input **daysSinceEntryExit**, then get out on the next session's open.

```
if daysSinceEntry = daysSinceEntryExit then
begin
```

```
   if mp = 1 then sell("LongBSEExit") next bar at open;
   if mp = -1 then buyToCover("ShortBSExit") next bar at open;
end;
```

Template2

EZ_Template2_5Min_PackBars - same as Template1, but uses the **PackDailyBars** function to extract historic data via arrays. This is a good place to demonstrate how the function works. A description of the inner workings of the function will be discussed in the next book. The first thing you must do is declare the arrays that you will be using with the function.

```
arrays: myOpen[30](0),myHigh[30](0),myLow[30](0),myClose[30](0);
```

Remember arrays are just lists that can be indexed. Instead of having 30 discrete myOpen variables (like myOpen1, myOpen2...) we utilize a list. Passing the list to a function is better than passing 30 variable names.

```
value99 =
   PackDailyBars(startTime,endTime,30,myOpen,myHigh,myLow,myClose,
      useSettlement,settlementTime,endTime);
```

Value99 is just a dummy variable. Functions need to be able to return and assign a value to a variable even if it is never used. Here is the *formal parameter* list for this cool function.

1.) **startTime** - time stamp of when to start collecting data. If you just want to collect and pack data from 9:00 a.m. TO 3:00 p.m. and treat this time span as a daily bar, then you would assign 900 to this variable name. In our example we are passing the **sessionStartTime**.

2.) **endTime** - in the example above you would pass it 1500, which is 3:00 p.m. In the template, **endTime** is set to the **sessionEndTime**.

3.) **numberOfDaysToStore** - in this example 30 days.

4 - 7.) **myOpen, myHigh, myLow, myClos**e - the receptacles that will hold the user specified number of days of data.

8.) **useSettlement** - False - in this case we are not worried about the settlement.

9.) **settlement time** - endTime - just use the **sessionEndTime** in this case.

endTime = **iff**(useSettlement,settlementTime,endTime);

If **useSettlment** is false, then the **sessionEndTime** is used in the function to trigger the collection of the close and to stop searching for the high and low extremes of the day.

10.) **settlementFormula** - which formula is used to determine settlement price if **useSettlement** is True.

    a.) close of the **settlementTime** bar
    b.) (high + low) / 2 of **settlementTime** bar
    c.) (high + low + close) / 3 of **settlementTime** bar

Once you pass this information to the function, the arrays **myOpen, myHigh**... are filled with **numberOfDaysToStore** daily bar data. Here is how you access the information to calculate a buy/ short entry or exit order.

stb = myHigh[1] + minMove/priceScale;
sts = myLow[1] - minMove/priceScale;

The arrays work their way backwards in time. Since we are on the last bar of the trading day all the historical daily bar values are shuffled down in the list. So my**High[1]** is the high of yesterday and **myHigh[2]** is the high of the day before to yesterday.

Template 3

EZ_ORBO_TEMPLATE_5MIN - the rest of the templates that solely use a single intraday bar data stream will incorporate the **packDailyBars** functionality. Since we have 30 days of historic data at our disposal, we can can easily calculate an 10-day average true range. The ATR calculation only takes place when there is valid data in **myClose[atrLen]**. This location in the **myClose** array only becomes non-zero when 30 days have been loaded into the array. Notice how the arrays are used in the ATR calculation and the determination of the up and down close patterns.

```
if firstDayComplete = True then
begin
   value99 =
   PackDailyBars(startTime,endTime,30,myOpen,myHigh,
   myLow,myClose,useSettlement,settlementTime,
   settlementFormula);
   if myClose[atrLen] <> 0 then
   begin
      atrSum = 0.0;
      for iCnt = 1 to atrLen
      begin
         atrSum = atrSum +
           maxList(myClose[iCnt+1],myHigh[iCnt])-
             minList(myClose[iCnt+1],myLow[iCnt]);
      end;
      atrVal = atrSum/atrLen;

      upClose = myClose[1] > myClose[2];
      dnClose = myClose[1] <= myClose[2];

             stb = openTick + harderBOPer * atrVal;
      sts = openTick - easierBOPer * atrVal;
      if upClose then
      begin
         value2 = value2 + 1;
         stb = openTick - easierBOPer * atrVal;
         sts = openTick - harderBOPer * atrVal;
      end;
   end;
end;
regCloseTime = True;
buysToday = 0;
shortsToday = 0;
```

```
myBarNumber = 0;
firstDayComplete = myClose[atrLen] <> 0;
```

FirstDayComplete only turns true when **myClose[atrLen]** has valid data. Once our daily bar arrays **(myHigh,myLow,...)** have been populated by at least **atrLen** days, then we can use that data to the same calculations that we originally did with **data2**. The buyEasierDay and shortEasierDays are now defined with **easierBOPer** and **harderBOPer** user inputs.

```
stb = openTick + harderBOPer * atrVal;
sts = openTick - easierBOPer * atrVal;
if upClose then
begin
   value2 = value2 + 1;
   stb =  openTick - easierBOPer * atrVal;
   sts =  openTick - harderBOPer * atrVal;
end;
```

That is all it took to incorporate longer term daily bar indicators into our algorithm. Keep in mind that the vast library of daily bar based indicators that TradeStation offers is still not available to charts that use just one intraday data stream. Just because we fill arrays with our home grown daily bars doesn't mean we can pass the array data to the indicator functions. All these indicators will need to be re-written to accept arrays in place of **numericSeries** such as EasyLanguage's **open, high, low, close** and their derivatives.

Template 4

EZ_VRBO_TEMPLATE1_5MIN

The main purpose of this template was two fold: 1) eliminate the use of **data2** and 2) see if we could get similar results while allowing executions on the very first bar of the day. This template uses the **packDailyBars** function to store historic daily bar values.

This template requires you to do calculations on the last trading bar of the day and also on the first bar of the trading day. Since we are daytrading, then you need to rest you **buysToday** and **shortsToday** to zero, and also continue doing your **DOW** analysis. Everything else that includes the pattern recognition, average true range calculation and long and short entry levels can be completed on the last bar of the day.

APPENDIX A-SOURCE CODE

This appendix includes all of the source code. This code will be made available on my website www.georgepruitt.com as an ELD and as text files. You can try and copy portions of this code and paste into the EL Editor, but there no guarantee it will Verify. The better practice is to open the HiResCode.txt and copy/aste from it.

```
//EZ_ORBO_DAILY BARS
//A Looks too good to be true algorithm
//Used for demonstration purposes only
// **** Danger Danger **** usin with LIB ONLY
if close > close[1] then
begin
    buy("Orbo20Buy") next bar at open of tomorrow + 0.20 * trueRange stop;
    sellShort("Orbo40Shrt") next bar at open of tomorrow - 0.40 * trueRange stop;
end
else
begin
    buy("Orbo40Buy") next bar at open of tomorrow + 0.40 * trueRange stop;
    sellShort("Orbo20Shrt") next bar at open of tomorrow - 0.20 * trueRange stop;
end;

setStopLoss(500);
setProfitTarget(1000);
```

$$\triangle\triangle\triangle$$

```
//EZ_ORBO_DAILY 5 min bars
//Intrabay testing template
//
//
inputs: useSettlement(True),settlementTime(1600),settlementFormula(1);
vars:
    openTick(0),
```

```
        buysToday(0),shortsToday(0),
        highOfDay1(0),lowOfDay1(0),
        closeOfDay1(0),closeOfDay2(0),
        firstDayComplete(False),
        mp(0),atrVal(0),myTR(0),
        regCloseTime(False),
        upClose(False),dnClose(False),
        myBarNumber(0),
        stb(0),sts(0),
        whichBar(0);

vars: startTime(0),endTime(0),startTimeOffset(0),endTimeOffSet(0);

startTime = sessionStartTime(0,1);
endTime   = sessionEndtime(0,1);

if t = sessionendTime(0,1) or (t < 2300 and time of next bar > calcTime(t,60)) then
begin
        openTick = open of next bar;
        if firstDayComplete = True then
        begin
            if useSettlement = False then closeOfDay1 = c;
            upClose = closeOfDay1 > closeOfDay2;
            dnClose = closeOfDay1 <= closeOfDay2;
            myTR = maxList(closeOfDay2,highOfDay1) -
                    minList(closeOfDay2,lowOfDay1);
            stb = openTick + 0.40 * myTR;
            sts =  openTick - 0.20 * myTR;
            if upClose then
            begin
                value2 = value2 + 1;
                stb = openTick + 0.20 * myTR;
                sts =  openTick - 0.40 * myTR;
             end;
             closeOfDay2 = closeOfDay1;
        end;
        regCloseTime = True;

        buysToday = 0;
        shortsToday = 0;
        myBarNumber = 0;
        highOfDay1 = maxList(h,highOfDay1);
        lowOfDay1 = minList(l,lowOfDay1);
        firstDayComplete = True;
end;

if t = StartTime + barInterval then
begin
        HighOfDay1 = 0;
        LowOfDay1  = 999999999;
end;

if startTime > endTime then
begin
```

```
        endTimeOffset = 0;
        if t >= startTime+barInterval and t<= 2359 then
            endTimeOffSet = 2400-endTime;
end;

mp = marketPosition;

if t-endTimeOffSet < endTime  then
begin
        if mp = 1 and mp[1] = 1 and totalTrades >value1 then buysToday = buysToday + 1;
        if mp = -1 and mp[1] =-1 and totalTrades >value1 then shortsToday=shortsToday+ 1;
        if mp = 0 and mp[1] = 0 and totalTrades > value1 then
        begin
            if l <= sts then shortsToday = shortsToday + 1;
            if h >= stb then buysToday = buysToday + 1;
        end;
        if mp = 1 and mp[1] <> 1 then buysToday = buysToday + 1;
        if mp =-1 and mp[1] <> -1 then shortsToday = shortsToday + 1;
        value1 = totalTrades;
end;

myBarNumber = myBarNumber + 1;

highOfDay1 = maxList(highOfDay1,high);
lowOfDay1 = minList(lowOfDay1,low);

if useSettlement then
begin
        condition1 = t = settlementTime;
        condition2 = t[1] < settlementTime and t > settlementTime;
        condition3 = t[1] < settlementTime and t < t[1];
        whichBar = 0;
        if condition2 or condition3 then
            whichBar = 1;
end;

if condition1 or condition2 or condition3 then
begin
        if settlementFormula = 1 then closeOfDay1 = c[whichBar]; // if using settle time tick
        if settlementFormula = 2 then closeOfDay1 = (h[whichBar] + l[whichBar])/2; // form.1
        if settlementFormula = 3 then
            closeOfDay1 = (c[whichBar]+ h[whichBar] + l[whichBar])/3; //form.2
end;

setStopLoss(500);
setProfitTarget(1000);

if firstDayComplete then
begin
        if upClose then
        begin
          stb = openTick + 0.20 * myTR;  //redundant - left in for clarification
          sts = openTick - 0.40 * myTR;
          stb = roundToNearestTick(stb,"Dn");
```

```
        sts = roundToNearestTick(sts,"Up");
            if buysToday = 0 and c <= stb then buy("Orbo20Buy") next bar at stb stop;
            if shortsToday = 0 and c >= sts then sellShort("Orbo40Shrt") next bar at sts stop;
    end
    else
    begin
        stb = openTick + 0.40 * myTR; //redundant - left in for clarification
        sts = openTick - 0.20 * myTR;
        stb = roundToNearestTick(stb,"Dn");
        sts = roundToNearestTick(sts,"Up");
            if buysToday = 0 and c <= stb then buy("Orbo40Buy") next bar at stb stop;
            if shortsToday = 0 and c >= sts then sellShort("Orbo20Shrt") next bar at sts stop;
    end;
end;
```

$$\triangle\triangle\triangle$$

```
//EZ_ORBO_DAILY 5 min bars using Data 2 - [daily bars]
//Intraday testing template
//
// set up order

vars:
    openTick(0),
    buysToday(0),shortsToday(0),
    highOfDay1(0),lowOfDay1(0),
    closeOfDay1(0),closeOfDay2(0),
    firstDayComplete(False),
    mp(0),atrVal(0),myTR(0),
    regCloseTime(False),
    upClose(False),dnClose(False),
    myBarNumber(0),
    stb(0),sts(0),holidayFound(False),holidayCnt(0);

vars: startTime(0),endTime(0),
      startTimeOffset(0),endTimeOffSet(0);

startTime = sessionStartTime(0,1);
endTime   = sessionEndtime(0,1);

if t = sessionStartTime(0,1) + barInterval or
    (t[1] < sessionStartTime(0,1) and t > sessionStartTime(0,1)+barInterval) then
begin
    holidayFound = False;
    closeofDay1 = close of data2;
    closeOfDay2 = close[1] of data2;
    if d > calcDate(d of data2,2) or
    (t > calcTime(t[1],65) and d = calcDate(d of data2,1)) or
    (t[1] = endTime and d = calcDate(d of data2,1)) then
    begin
```

```
            holidayFound = True;
            holidayCnt = holidayCnt + 1;
            if t[1] <> endTime and d = d[1] then
            begin
                closeofDay2 = closeOfDay1;
                closeOfDay1=c[1];
            end;
            myTr = maxList(closeOfDay2,highOfDay1) - minList(closeOfDay2,lowOfDay1);
        end
        else
        begin
            myTR = trueRange of data2;
        end;
        openTick = open;
        upClose = closeofday1 > closeofday2;
        dnClose = closeofday1 <= closeofday2;
        stb = openTick + 0.40 * myTR;
        sts =  openTick - 0.20 * myTR;
        if upClose then
        begin
            value2 = value2 + 1;
            stb = openTick + 0.20 * myTR;
          sts =  openTick - 0.40 * myTR;
        end;
        if upClose then value2 = value2 + 1;

        buysToday = 0;
        shortsToday = 0;
        myBarNumber = 0;
        highOfDay1 = 0;
        lowOfDay1 = 999999999;
        highOfDay1 = maxList(h,highOfDay1);
        lowOfDay1 = minList(l,lowOfDay1);
end;


if t >=StartTime and t[1] < StartTime then StartTimeOffSet = 0;
EndTimeOffSet = 0;
if t>=StartTime and t < 2359 then EndTimeOffSet = 2400 - EndTime;
if t < t[1] then StartTimeOffSet = 2400;


mp = marketPosition;


if t+StartTimeOffset>startTime and t-endTimeOffSet < endTime  then
begin
    if mp = 1 and mp[1] = 1 and totalTrades > value1 then buysToday = buysToday + 1;
    if mp =-1 and mp[1] =-1 and totalTrades > value1 then shortsToday=shortsToday + 1;
    if mp = 0 and mp[1] = 0 and totalTrades > value1 then
    begin
        if l <= sts then shortsToday = shortsToday + 1;
        if h >= stb then buysToday = buysToday + 1;
    end;
    if mp = 1 and mp[1] <> 1 then begin
```

```
            buysToday = buysToday + 1;
        end;
        if mp =-1 and mp[1] <> -1 then
        begin
            shortsToday = shortsToday + 1;
        end;
        value1 = totalTrades;
end;
myBarNumber = myBarNumber + 1;


if t <> sessionendTime(0,1) then
begin
    if upClose then
    begin
        if buysToday = 0 and c <= stb  then buy("Orbo20Buy") next bar at stb stop;
        if shortsToday = 0 and c >= sts then sellShort("Orbo40Shrt") next bar at sts stop;
    end
    else
    begin
        if buysToday = 0 and c <= stb then buy("Orbo40Buy") next bar at stb stop;
        if shortsToday = 0 and c >= sts then sellShort("Orbo20Shrt") next bar at sts stop;
    end;
end;


setStopLoss(500);
setProfitTarget(1000);
```

ΔΔΔ

```
// Daytrading system using support and resistance levels
// Pattern recognition thru ANDING consecutive Booleans values
// Use of Enumeration for iterative purposes

vars:pvtPrice(0),r1(0),r2(0),r3(0),s1(0),s2(0),s3(0);
inputs: lastEntryTime(1530),profitObj$(1000),stopLoss$(500);;
vars:
buysToday(0),shortsToday(0);
vars: stateA(0),stateB(0);

if d <> d[1] then
begin
    buysToday = 0;
    shortsToday = 0;
    pvtPrice = (high of data2 + close of data2 + low of data2) / 3 ;
    r1 = 2 * pvtPrice - low of data2;
    r2 = pvtPrice + (high of data2 - low of data2);
    r3 = high of data2 + 2 * (pvtPrice - low of data2);
    s1 = 2 * pvtPrice - high of data2;
    s2 = pvtPrice - (high of data2 - low of data2);
    s3 = low of data2 - 2 * (high of data2 - pvtPrice);
```

```
        stateA = 0;
        stateB = 0;
        if open > r3 then print(d," ",t," "," market gapped above r3 ",open," ",r3);
end;
if t < 1530 then
begin
    if buysToday  = 0 then
    begin
            if openD(0) > r2 and close crosses above r3 then
            begin
                buy("R3-BO") next bar at open;
                buysToday = buysToday + 1;
            end;
            if stateB = 0 and openD(0) < pvtPrice and openD(0) > s1 then
                stateB = 1;

            if stateB = 1 and close crosses below s2 then
                stateB = 2;

            if stateb = 2 and close crosses above s1 then
                stateB = 3;

            if stateB = 3 then
            begin
                stateB = 999;buysToday = buysToday + 1;
                buy("S2rev@S1") next bar at open;
            end;
    end;
    if shortsToday = 0 then
    begin
            if stateA = 0 and openD(0) > pvtPrice  and openD(0) < r1 then
                stateA = 1;

            if stateA = 1 and close crosses above r2 then
                stateA = 2;

            if stateA = 2 and close crosses below r1 then
                stateA = 3;

            if stateA = 3 then
            begin
                stateA = 0;shortsToday = shortsToday + 1;
                sellShort("R2rev@R1") next bar at open;
            end;

            if  openD(0) < s2 and close crosses below s3 then
            begin
                sellShort("S3-BO") next bar at open;
                shortsToday = shortsToday + 1;
            end;
    end;
end;
SetStopPosition;
setProfitTarget(profitObj$);
```

```
setStopLoss(stopLoss$);
setExitOnClose;
```

△△△

```
inputs:
lastEntryTime(1530),buyBOLevels(1),shortBOLevels(1),
buyRevLevels(1),shortRevLevels(1),tradeFilter(1),atrLen(10),nrLen(7),
useVolExits(True),perOfATRProfObj(1.2),perOfATRStopLoss(.56),
profitObj$(1300),stopLoss$(900);

vars:
buysToday(0),shortsToday(0), stateA(0),stateB(0),pvtPrice(0),
r1(0),r2(0),r3(0),s1(0),s2(0),s3(0);

vars:
buyBOLev1(0),buyBOLev2(0),shortBOLev1(0),shortBOLev2(0),
buyRevLev1(0),buyRevLev2(0),buyRevLev3(0),
shortRevLev1(0),shortRevLev2(0),shortRevLev3(0);

vars:
ATRValue(0),ATRMin(0),canTrade(False);


if d <> d[1] then
begin
    buysToday = 0;
    shortsToday = 0;
    pvtPrice = (high of data2 + close of data2 + low of data2) / 3 ;
    r1 = 2 * pvtPrice - low of data2;
    r2 = pvtPrice + (high of data2 - low of data2);
    r3 = high of data2 + 2 * (pvtPrice - low of data2);
    s1 = 2 * pvtPrice - high of data2;
    s2 = pvtPrice - (high of data2 - low of data2);
    s3 = low of data2 - 2 * (high of data2 - pvtPrice);
    stateA = 0;
    stateB = 0;
    ATRValue = avgTrueRange(atrLen) of data2;
    ATRMin = lowest(truerange of data2,nrLen);

end;

//enumerate the universe of different volatility filters
canTrade = False;

if tradeFilter = 1 then
begin
    canTrade = truerange of data2 < ATRValue;
end;
```

```
if tradeFilter = 2 then
begin
     canTrade = trueRange of data2 = ATRMin;
end;
if tradeFilter = 3 then
begin
     canTrade = trueRange of data2 > ATRValue;
end;


//enumerate the universe of different Buy Break Outs
if buyBOLevels = 1 then
begin
     buyBOLev1 = r2;
     buyBOLev2 = r3;
end;
if buyBOLevels = 2 then
begin
     buyBOLev1 = r1;
     buyBOLev2 = r2;
end;
if buyBOLevels = 3 then
begin
     buyBOLev1 = pvtPrice;
     buyBOLev2 = r1;
end;

//enumerate the universe of different Short Break Outs
if shortBOLevels = 1 then
begin
     shortBOLev1 = s2;
     shortBOLev2 = s3;
end;
if shortBOLevels = 2 then
begin
     shortBOLev1 = s1;
     shortBOLev2 = s2;
end;
if shortBOLevels = 3 then
begin
     shortBOLev1 = pvtPrice;
     shortBOLev2 = s1;
end;
if shortBOLevels = 4 then
begin
     shortBOLev1 = r1;
     shortBOLev2 = s2;
end;

//enumerate the universe of different Long Reversals

if buyRevLevels = 1 then
begin
     buyRevLev1 = pvtPrice;
```

```
        buyRevLev2 = s1;
        buyRevLev3 = s2;
end;

if buyRevLevels = 2 then
begin
        buyRevLev1 = s1;
        buyRevLev2 = s2;
        buyRevLev3 = s3;
end;

if buyRevLevels = 3 then
begin
        buyRevLev1 = s2;
        buyRevLev2 = s3;
        buyRevLev3 = s3;
end;

//enumerate the universe of different Long Reversals

if shortRevLevels = 1 then
begin
        shortRevLev1 = pvtPrice;
        shortRevLev2 = r1;
        shortRevLev3 = r2;
end;

if shortRevLevels = 2 then
begin
        shortRevLev1 = r1;
        shortRevLev2 = r2;
        shortRevLev3 = r3;
end;

if shortRevLevels = 3 then
begin
        shortRevLev1 = r2;
        shortRevLev2 = r3;
        shortRevLev3 = r3;
end;

if  t < 1530 and canTrade then
begin
        if buysToday = 0 then
        begin
        // BUY break out trades section
            if openD(0) > buyBOLev1 and close crosses above buyBOLev2 then
            begin
                buy("RLevel-BO") next bar at open;
                buysToday = buysToday + 1;
            end;
        // BUY reversal trades section
            if stateB = 0 and openD(0) < buyRevLev1 and openD(0) > buyRevLev2 then
                stateB = 1;
```

```
            if stateB = 1 and close crosses below buyRevLev3 then
                stateB = 2;

            if stateb = 2 and close crosses above buyRevLev2 then
                stateB = 3;

            if stateB = 3 then
            begin
                stateB = 999;
                buy("+LLevel-REV") next bar at open;
                buysToday = buysToday + 1;
            end;
        end;
        if shortsToday = 0 then
        begin
        // SHORT break out trades section
            if openD(0) < shortBOLev1 and close crosses below shortBOLev2 then
            begin
                sellShort("SLevel-BO") next bar at open;
                shortsToday = shortsToday + 1;
            end;

        // SHORT reversal trades section
            if stateA = 0 and openD(0) > shortRevLev1 and openD(0) < shortRevLev2 then
                stateA = 1;

            if stateA = 1 and close crosses above shortRevLev3 then
                stateA = 2;

            if stateA = 2 and close crosses below shortRevLev2 then
                stateA = 3;

            if stateA = 3 then
            begin
                stateA = 0;
                sellShort("+SLevel-REV") next bar at open;
                PRINT(D," ",T," +SLevel-REV");
                shortsToday = shortsToday + 1;
            end;
        end;
    end;
end;


SetStopPosition;

if useVolExits then
begin
    if currentShares > 0 then
    begin
        setProfitTarget(perOfAtrProfObj*ATRValue*bigPointValue*currentShares);
        setStopLoss(perOfAtrStopLoss*ATRValue*bigPointValue*currentShares);
    end;
end
else
```

```
begin
    setProfitTarget(profitObj$);
    setStopLoss(stopLoss$);
end;

setExitOnClose;
```

△△△

```
inputs:profitObj$(1320),stopLoss$(900),useVolExits(False),
perOfATRProfObj(2.05),perOfATRStopLoss(1.05),
useTrailPercentStop(True),trailPercentThresh$(750),trailPercent(0.5),
barCountDelay(1),offsetPer1(.15),offsetPer2(.3),
tradePatternNum(1),closePatternNum(1),openPatternNum(1),
atrLen(10),atrMult(1),nrLen(7),reverseOnStopLoss(True),
reversalTimeBase(1100),reversalTimeIncrement(70);

vars:stb(0),sts(0),zatr(0),myBarCount(0),
    buyEasierDay(False),shortEasierDay(False);

vars:buysToday(0),sellsToday(0),mp(0),totTrades(0),
    tradePattMatch(False),buyPattMatch(False),shortPattMatch(False);

vars:MProf(0),TProf(0),WProf(0),RProf(0),FProf(0),
    begDayEquity(0),endDayEquity(0);

vars: loss$(0),prof$(0);

//print(date," ",date[1]);

vars: pattString("");

if date <> date[1] then
begin
    myBarCount = 0;
    buysToday = 0;sellsToday = 0;
    zatr = avgTrueRange(atrLen) of data2;

    loss$ = stopLoss$;
    prof$ = profitObj$;
    if useVolExits then
    begin
        loss$ = perOfATRStopLoss * zatr * bigPointValue;
        prof$ = perOfATRProfObj * zatr * bigPointValue;
//      loss$ = minList(loss$,2000);
//      prof$ = minList(prof$,4000);
    end;


//   print(d,pattString);
```

163

```
    if totalTrades > totTrades then
    begin
        switch(dayOfWeek(date[1]))
        begin
            Case 1: MProf = MProf + (netProfit - begDayEquity);
            Case 2: TProf = TProf + (netProfit - begDayEquity);
            Case 3: WProf = WProf + (netProfit - begDayEquity);
            Case 4: RProf = RProf + (netProfit - begDayEquity);
            Case 5: FProf = FProf + (netProfit - begDayEquity);
            Default: Value1 = Value1 + 1;
        end;
        begDayEquity = netProfit;

    end;
    totTrades = totalTrades;
    switch(tradePatternNum)
    begin
        Case 1:
            condition1 = range of data2 < zatr *atrMult;
        Case 2:
            condition1 = range of data2 >= zatr *atrMult;
        Case 3:
            condition1 = range of data2 = lowest(range of data2,nrLen);
        Default:
            condition1 = False;
    end;
    switch(closePatternNum)
    begin
        Case 1:
            buyPattMatch = close of data2 >= close[1] of Data2;
            shortPattMatch = close of data2 < close[1] of Data2;
        Case 2:
            buyPattMatch = close of data2 < close[1] of Data2;
            shortPattMatch = close of data2 >= close[1] of Data2;
        Default:
            buyPattMatch = False;
            shortPattMatch = False;
    end;
    switch(openPatternNum)
    begin
        Case 1:
            buyPattMatch =  buyPattMatch and open >= close of data2;
            shortPattMatch = shortPattMatch and open < close of data2;
        Case 2:
            buyPattMatch =  buyPattMatch and open < close of data2;
            shortPattMatch = shortPattMatch and open >= close of data2;
        Default:
            buyPattMatch = False;
            shortPattMatch = False;
    end;
//   if buyPattMatch or shortPattMatch then print(d," buyPattMatch ",buyPattMatch," shortPattMatch
",shortPattMatch);
end;
```

```
myBarCount = myBarCount + 1;
if time > 1530 then condition1 = false;
mp = marketPosition;
buyEasierDay = False;
shortEasierDay = False;


if buyPattMatch then buyEasierDay = True;
if shortPattMatch then shortEasierDay = True;

if buyEasierDay then
begin
    stb = openD(0) + offsetPer1 * zatr;
    sts = openD(0) - offsetPer2 * zatr;
end;

if shortEasierDay then
begin
    stb = openD(0) + offsetPer2 * zatr;
    sts = openD(0) - offsetPer1 * zatr;
end;

if mp[1] <> 1 and mp = 1 then buysToday = buysToday + 1;
if mp[1] <>-1 and mp = -1 then sellsToday = sellsToday + 1;
if mp[1] = 0 and mp = 0 and
totalTrades > totTrades and h >= stb then
    buysToday = buysToday + 1;
if mp[1] = 0 and mp = 0 and
totalTrades > totTrades and l <= sts then
    buysToday = buysToday + 1;

if myBarCount > barCountDelay and t < sessionEndTime(0,1) and condition1 and
(buyEasierDay or shortEasierDay)  then
begin
    if buysToday = 0 {and c < stb} then buy("BBo") next bar at stb stop;
    if sellsToday = 0 {and c > sts} then sellshort("SBo") next bar at sts stop;
end;


if marketPosition = 1 and reverseOnStopLoss and sellsToday = 0 and
    time < calcTime(reversalTimeBase,reversalTimeIncrement) then
    sellshort("RevShrt") next bar at entryPrice - loss$/bigPointValue stop;
if marketPosition =-1 and reverseOnStopLoss and buysToday = 0 and
    time < calcTime(reversalTimeBase,reversalTimeIncrement) then
    buy("RevLong") next bar at entryPrice + loss$/bigPointValue stop;

if marketPosition = 1 then sell("LongXit") next bar at entryPrice - loss$/bigPointValue stop;
if marketPosition =-1 then buytocover("ShrtXit") next bar at entryPrice + loss$/bigPointValue stop;

if useTrailPercentStop then
begin
    if marketPosition = 1 then
    begin
        if maxPositionProfit > trailPercentThresh$ then
```

```
            sell("LongTrail") next bar at
                entryPrice + (1-trailPercent)* maxPositionProfit/bigPointValue stop;
    end;
    if marketPosition = -1 then
    begin
        if maxPositionProfit > trailPercentThresh$ then
            buyToCover("ShortTrail") next bar at
                entryPrice - (1-trailPercent)* maxPositionProfit/bigPointValue stop;
    end;
end;


if marketPosition = 1 then sell("LongProf") next bar at
    entryPrice + prof$/bigPointValue limit;
if marketPosition =-1 then buytocover("ShrtProf") next bar at
    entryPrice - prof$/bigPointValue limit;

if d = 1211027 and t = 1100 then
begin
    print(d," DOW Analysis ");
    print("Monday    : ",MProf);
    print("Tuesday   : ",TProf);
    print("Wednesday : ",WProf);
    print("Thursday  : ",RProf);
    print("Friday    : ",FProf);

end;

setExitOnClose;
```

ΔΔΔ

```
{EZ- Camarilla Pyramid Framework Using Day Session or Equities
Data1: Plot on 5 min or less time frame.
Data2: Daily}


inputs:
lastEntryTime(1530),numSharesCons(1),numBarsToWait(3),
buyBOLevels(1),shortBOLevels(1),
buyRevLevels(2),shortRevLevels(2),tradeFilter(1),atrLen(10),nrLen(7),
useVolExits(False),perOfATRProfObj(1.2),perOfATRStopLoss(.56),
useTrailPercentStop(False),trailPercentThresh$(500),trailPercent(0.3),
profitObj$(1950),stopLoss$(1450),maxLongEntries(2),maxShortEntries(2);

vars:
buysToday(0),shortsToday(0), stateA(0),stateB(0),pvtPrice(0),
r1(0),r2(0),r3(0),r4(0),s1(0),s2(0),s3(0),s4(0);

vars:
```

```
buyBOLev1(0),buyBOLev2(0),shortBOLev1(0),shortBOLev2(0),
buyRevLev1Str(""),buyRevLev2Str(""),buyRevLev3Str(""),
buyRevLev1(0),buyRevLev2(0),buyRevLev3(0),
shortRevLev1Str(""),shortRevLev2Str(""),shortRevLev3Str(""),
shortRevLev1(0),shortRevLev2(0),shortRevLev3(0),
totTrades(0),waitBar(0),minTick(0);
vars: s2Buy(False),s3Buy(False);
vars:
ATRValue(0),ATRMin(0),canTrade(False);

vars: thePath(""),numCrossings(0);

vars: myClose(0),myHigh(0),myLow(0);
vars: buyLevel(0),mp(0),curShares(0);
vars:highOfMaxLongProf(0),lowOfMaxShortProf(0),priorMaxPosProf(0);
if time = sessionStartTime(0,1)+barInterval then
begin
    myClose = close of data2;
    myHigh = high of data2;
    myLow = low of data2;

//  myClose = closeD(1);
//  myHigh = highD(1);
//  myLow = lowD(1);


    buysToday = 0;
    shortsToday = 0;
    s2Buy = False;
    s3Buy = False;



    r4 = myClose+(myHigh-myLow) * 1.1 / 2;
    r3 = myClose+(myHigh-myLow) * 1.1/4;
    r2 = myClose+(myHigh-myLow) * 1.1/6;
    r1 = myClose+(myHigh-myLow) * 1.1/12;
    s1 = myClose-(myHigh-myLow) * 1.1/12;
    s2 = myClose-(myHigh-myLow) * 1.1/6;
    s3 = myClose-(myHigh-myLow) * 1.1/4;
    s4 = myClose-(myHigh-myLow) * 1.1/2;

    minTick = minMove/priceScale;

    R1 = R1 - (mod(R1,minTick));
    R2 = R2 - (mod(R2,minTick));
    R3 = R3 - (mod(R3,minTick));
    R4 = R4 - (mod(R4,minTick));

    S4 = S4 + (minTick-mod(S4,minTick));
    S3 = S3 + (minTick-mod(S3,minTick));
    S2 = S2 + (minTick-mod(S2,minTick));
    S1 = S1 + (minTick-mod(S1,minTick));
```

```
waitBar = 0;

stateA = 0;
stateB = 0;

ATRValue = avgTrueRange(atrLen) of data2;
ATRMin = lowest(truerange of data2,nrLen);

if tradeFilter = 0 then canTrade = True;

if tradeFilter = 1 then
begin
    canTrade = truerange of data2 < ATRValue;
end;
if tradeFilter = 2 then
begin
    canTrade = trueRange of data2 = ATRMin;
end;
if tradeFilter = 3 then
begin
    canTrade = trueRange of data2 > ATRValue;
end;

if buyBOLevels = 1 then
begin
    buyBOLev1 = r4;
end;
if shortBOLevels = 1 then
begin
    shortBoLev2 = s4;
end;

if buyRevLevels = 1 then
begin
    buyRevLev1Str = "-s2";
    buyRevLev1 = s2;
    buyRevLev2Str = "-s3";
    buyRevLev2 = s3;
    buyRevLev3Str = "-s4";
    buyRevLev3 = s4;
end;

if buyRevLevels = 2 then
begin
    buyRevLev1Str = "-s1";
    buyRevLev1 = s1;
    buyRevLev2Str = "-s2";
    buyRevLev2 = s2;
    buyRevLev3Str = "-s3";
    buyRevLev3 = s3;
end;
if buyRevLevels <> 1 and buyRevLevels <> 2 then
begin
    buyRevLev1Str = "zzz";
```

```
        buyRevLev1 = s1;
        buyRevLev2Str = "zzz";
        buyRevLev2 = s2;
        buyRevLev3Str = "zzz";
        buyRevLev3 = s3;
    end;

    //enumerate the universe of different Long Reversals
    if shortRevLevels = 1 then
    begin
        shortRevLev1Str = "+r2";
        shortRevLev1 = r2;
        shortRevLev2Str = "+r3";
        shortRevLev2 = r3;
        shortRevLev3Str = "+r4";
        shortRevLev3 = r4;
    end;
    if shortRevLevels = 2 then
    begin
        shortRevLev1Str = "+r1";
        shortRevLev1 = r1;
        shortRevLev2Str = "+r2";
        shortRevLev2 = r2;
        shortRevLev3Str = "+r3";
        shortRevLev3 = r3;
    end;
    if shortRevLevels <> 1 and shortRevLevels <> 2 then
    begin
        shortRevLev1Str = "zzz";
        shortRevLev1 = r1;
        shortRevLev2Str = "zzz";
        shortRevLev2 = r2;
        shortRevLev3Str = "zzz";
        shortRevLev3 = r3;
    end;
    totTrades = totalTrades;
    thePath = "";
    numCrossings = 0;
end;

waitBar = waitBar + 1;

if waitBar > numBarsToWait then
begin

    if h crosses above r1 then thePath = thePath + "+r1";
    if h crosses above r2 then thePath = thePath + "+r2";
    if h crosses above r3 then thePath = thePath + "+r3";
    if h crosses above r4 then thePath = thePath + "+r4";
    if h crosses above s1 then thePath = thePath + "+s1";
    if h crosses above s2 then thePath = thePath + "+s2";
    if h crosses above 23 then thePath = thePath + "+s3";
    if h crosses above s4 then thePath = thePath + "+s4";
```

```
        if l crosses below r1 then thePath = thePath + "-r1";
        if l crosses below r2 then thePath = thePath + "-r2";
        if l crosses below r3 then thePath = thePath + "-r3";
        if l crosses below r4 then thePath = thePath + "-r4";
        if l crosses below s1 then thePath = thePath + "-s1";
        if l crosses below s2 then thePath = thePath + "-s2";
        if l crosses below s3 then thePath = thePath + "-s3";
        if l crosses below s4 then thePath = thePath + "-s4";
        //if d = 1211208 then print(d," ",t," ",waitBar," ",thePath);
end;

numCrossings = strLen(thePath)/3;

mp = marketPosition;

if mp[1] <> 1 and mp = 1 then buysToday = buysToday + currentShares;

if mp[1] = mp and mp = 1 and currentShares > curShares then
    buysToday = buysToday + currentShares - curShares;

if mp[1] <>-1 and mp = -1 then shortsToday = shortsToday + currentShares;

if mp[1] = -1 and mp = -1 and currentShares > curShares then
    shortsToday = shortsToday + currentShares - curShares;

if time < lastEntryTime and waitBar > numBarsToWait and canTrade  then
begin
    if buyBOLevels <> 0 then
    begin
        if h < buyBOLev1 then buy("BBO") next bar a buyBOLev1 stop;
    end;
    if shortBOLevels <> 0 then
    begin
        if l > shortBOLev1 then sellShort("SBO") next bar a shortBOLev1 stop;
    end;

    if buyRevLev1Str <> "zzz" then
    begin
        if inStr(thePath,buyRevLev1Str) = 0 and l > buyRevLev1 and
        buysToday/numSharesCons < maxLongEntries then
            buy("SLevABuy") numSharesCons shares next bar at buyRevLev1 limit;
        if inStr(thePath,buyRevLev2Str) = 0 and l >  buyRevLev2 and
        buysToday/numSharesCons < maxLongEntries then
            buy("SLevBBuy") numSharesCons shares next bar at buyRevLev2 limit;
        if inStr(thePath,buyRevLev3Str) = 0 and l >  buyRevLev3 and
        buysToday/numSharesCons < maxLongEntries then
            buy("SLevCBuy") numSharesCons shares next bar at buyRevLev3 limit;
    end;
    if shortRevLev1Str <> "zzz" then
    begin
        if inStr(thePath,shortRevLev1Str) = 0 and h < shortRevLev1 and
        shortsToday/numSharesCons < maxShortEntries then
            sellShort("RLevAShort") numSharesCons shares next bar at shortRevLev1 limit;
        if inStr(thePath,shortRevLev2Str) = 0 and h < shortRevLev2 and
```

```
            shortsToday/numSharesCons < maxShortEntries then
            sellShort("RLevBShort") numSharesCons shares next bar at shortRevLev2 limit;
            if inStr(thePath,shortRevLev3Str) = 0 and h < shortRevLev3 and
            shortsToday/numSharesCons < maxShortEntries then
                sellShort("RLevCShort") numSharesCons shares next bar at shortRevLev3 limit;
      end;
end;

curShares = currentShares;
SetStopPosition;
if useTrailPercentStop then
begin
    if marketPosition = 1 then
    begin
        if maxPositionProfit > trailPercentThresh$ then
        begin
            sell("LongTrail") next bar at
                avgEntryPrice + (1 - trailPercent)  *
                maxPositionProfit/bigPointValue/currentShares stop;
        end;
    end;
    if marketPosition = -1 then
    begin
        if maxPositionProfit >  trailPercentThresh$ then
            buyToCover("ShortTrail") next bar at
                avgEntryPrice + (1 - trailPercent) *
                maxPositionProfit/bigPointValue/currentShares stop;
    end;
end;
if useVolExits then
begin
    if currentShares > 0 then
    begin
        setProfitTarget(perOfAtrProfObj*ATRValue*bigPointValue*currentShares);
        setStopLoss(perOfAtrStopLoss*ATRValue*bigPointValue*currentShares);
    end;
end
else
begin
    setProfitTarget(profitObj$);
    setStopLoss(stopLoss$);
end;
// Uncomment following line to print out the path of the day
 if t = sessionEndTime(0,1) and d = 1211208 then print(d," ",thePath);
//if marketPosition = 1 and
// currentShares = 2 then print(d," ",t," two long ",entryPrice," ",entryPrice(1));

priorMaxPosProf = maxPositionProfit;
setExitOnClose;
```

```
inputs: startTradeTime(700),startTradeTimeOffSet(5),
endTradeTime(2100),endTradeTimeOffSet(5),
numSharesCons(2),scaleOutAmt(1),
movAvgLen(100),momentumLen(10),offsetPer1(.4),
profitObj1$(500),profitObj2$(1000),stopLoss$(500),
useVolExits(True),
perOfATRProfObj1(2.05),perOfAtrProfObj2(3),perOfATRStopLoss(1.05),
tradeFilter(0),atrLen(10),atrMult(1),nrLen(7);

vars:stb(0),sts(0),zatr(0),myBarCount(0),ATRValue(0),ATRMin(0),
     openTick(0),trendFilter(0),momFilter(0);
vars:buysToday(0),shortsToday(0),mp(0),totTrades(0),totDailyTrades(0),
     startTime(0),startTimeOffSet(0),endTime(0),endTimeOffSet(0);

vars:MProf(0),TProf(0),WProf(0),RProf(0),FProf(0),
     begDayEquity(0),endDayEquity(0),curShares(0),canTrade(False);

vars: loss$(0),profit1$(0),profit2$(0),switchValue(0);

startTime = sessionStartTime(0,1);
endTime   = sessionEndtime(0,1);

endTimeOffSet = 0;
if t = calcTime(startTime,barInterval) then
begin
     openTick = open;
     if totalTrades > totDailyTrades then
     begin
       switchValue = iff(currentShares = 0,entryDate(1),entryDate(0));
          switch(dayOfWeek(switchValue))
          begin
               Case 1: MProf = MProf + (netProfit - begDayEquity);
               Case 2: TProf = TProf + (netProfit - begDayEquity);
               Case 3: WProf = WProf + (netProfit - begDayEquity);
               Case 4: RProf = RProf + (netProfit - begDayEquity);
               Case 5: FProf = FProf + (netProfit - begDayEquity);
               Default: Value1 = Value1 + 1;
          end;
          begDayEquity = netProfit;
          totDailyTrades = totalTrades;
     end;
     ATRValue = avgTrueRange(atrLen) of data2;
     ATRMin = lowest(truerange of data2,nrLen);
     trendFilter = iff(close of data2 > average(c,100),1,-1);
     momFilter = iff(close of data2 - close[momentumLen] of data2 > 0,1,-1);

     if tradeFilter = 0 then canTrade = True;

     if tradeFilter = 1 then
     begin
          canTrade = truerange of data2 < ATRValue;
     end;
     if tradeFilter = 2 then
```

```
    begin
        canTrade = trueRange of data2 = ATRMin;
    end;
    if tradeFilter = 3 then
    begin
        canTrade = trueRange of data2 > ATRValue;
    end;
end;

if calcTime(startTradeTime,startTradeTimeOffSet) >
calcTime(endTradeTime,endTradeTimeOffSet) then
begin
    endTimeOffset = 0;
    if t >= calcTime(startTradeTime,startTradeTimeOffSet) and t<= 2359 then
        endTimeOffSet = 2400-endTradeTime;
end;


if t = calcTime(startTradeTime,startTradeTimeOffSet) then
begin
    myBarCount = 0;
    buysToday = 0;
    shortsToday = 0;
    stb = roundToNearestTick(openTick + offSetPer1 * ATRValue,"Up");
    sts = roundToNearestTick(openTick - offSetPer1 * ATRValue,"Down");
    loss$ = stopLoss$;
    profit1$ = profitObj1$;
    print(d," ",t," first bar of trading window ",profit1$);
    profit2$ = profitObj2$;
    if useVolExits then
    begin
        loss$ = perOfATRStopLoss * ATRValue * bigPointValue * numSharesCons;
        profit1$ = perOfATRProfObj1 * ATRValue * bigPointValue *
                    (numSharesCons - scaleOutAmt) ;
        profit2$ = perOfATRProfObj2 * ATRValue * bigPointValue* scaleOutAmt;
    end;
end;
myBarCount = myBarCount + 1;
mp = marketPosition;
if mp = mp[1] and totalTrades > totTrades then
begin
    if h >= stb then buysToday = buysToday+numSharesCons;
    if l <= sts then shortsToday = shortsToday+numSharesCons;
end;
if mp[1] <> 1 and mp = 1 then buysToday = buysToday + currentShares;
if mp[1] = mp and mp = 1 and currentShares > curShares then
    buysToday = buysToday + currentShares - curShares;
if mp[1] <>-1 and mp = -1 then shortsToday = shortsToday + currentShares;
if mp[1] = -1 and mp = -1 and currentShares > curShares then
    shortsToday = shortsToday + currentShares - curShares;


if  t>=calcTime(startTradeTime,startTradeTimeOffSet) and t <
    minList(calcTime(endTradeTime,endTradeTimeOffSet),endTime) then
```

173

```
begin
    if trendFilter = 1 and momFilter = -1 and canTrade and
    currentShares = 0 and buysToday/numSharesCons =0 then
        buy("InitBuy") numSharesCons shares next bar at stb stop;

    if trendFilter = -1 and momFilter = 1 and canTrade and
    currentShares = 0 and shortsToday/numSharesCons = 0 then
        sellShort("InitShort") numSharesCons shares next bar at sts stop;
end;

if mp = 1 then
begin
    if currentShares = numSharesCons then
        sell("L-Prof1") scaleOutAmt shares next bar at
            roundToNearestTick(entryPrice + profit1$/bigPointValue,"Down") limit;
    if currentShares = numSharesCons - scaleOutAmt then
    begin
            L-BEven") next bar entryPrice stop;
        sell("L-Prof2") next bar at
            roundToNearestTick(entryPrice + profit2$/bigPointValue,"Down") limit;
    end;
//    if barsSinceEntry > 15 then sell next bar at open;
end;
if mp = -1 then
begin
    if currentShares = numSharesCons then
        buyToCover("S-Prof1") scaleOutAmt shares next bar at
            roundToNearestTick(entryPrice - profit1$/bigPointValue,"Up") limit;
    if currentShares = numSharesCons - scaleOutAmt then
    begin
            buyToCover("S-BEven") next bar entryPrice stop;
            buyToCover("S-Prof2") next bar at roundToNearestTick(entryPrice + profit2$/bigPoint-
Value,"Up") limit;
    end;
//    if barsSinceEntry > 15 then sell next bar at open;
end;

if d = 1211124 and t = 1100 then
begin
    print(d," DOW Analysis ");
    print("Monday   : ",MProf);
    print("Tuesday  : ",TProf);
    print("Wednesday : ",WProf);
    print("Thursday  : ",RProf);
    print("Friday   : ",FProf);

end;

totTrades = totalTrades;
curShares = currentShares;
SetStopPosition;
setStopLoss(loss$);
setExitOnClose;
```

$$\triangle\triangle\triangle$$

```
// using single FSM to control long and short entries
// lilBug is the current state of the market action
// looking to buy on retracement after RSI moves from oversold
// looking to short on rally after RSI moves from overBot

inputs: bugStartTime(930),bugStartTimeOffSet(60),
    bugEndTime(1545),bugEndTimeOffSet(-5),
    bugDropRisePer(0.4),rsiLen(3),
    bugOverBot(70),bugOverSold(30),
    numTrigBars(5),butterflyLife(5),numSharesCons(1),
    profitObj$(500),stopLoss$(500),
        useVolExits(True),atrLen(10),
        perOfATRProfObj(1.2),perOfATRStopLoss(0.6);


vars: lilBug(""),
lilBugPeak(0),lilBugValley(0),
lilBugPeakTime(0),lilBugValleyTime(0);
vars: mp(0);
vars: startTime(0),endTime(0),ATRValue(0);
vars: loss$(0),profit$(0);

startTime = calcTime(sessionStartTime(0,1),barInterval);
endTime = sessionEndTime(0,1);

if time = startTime then
begin
    ATRValue = avgTrueRange(atrLen) of data2;
    lilBug = "";
    loss$ = stopLoss$;
    profit$ = profitObj$;
    if useVolExits then
    begin
        loss$ = perOfATRStopLoss * ATRValue * bigPointValue * numSharesCons;
        profit$ = perOfATRProfObj * ATRValue * bigPointValue * numSharesCons ;
    end;
end;


mp = marketPosition;

if time = calcTime(bugStartTime,bugStartTimeOffSet) then
begin
    lilBug = "worm";
    lilBugPeak = h;
    lilBugPeakTime = t;
    lilBugValley = l;
    lilBugValleyTime = t;
end;
```

```
switch (lilBug)
begin
    case("worm"):
        if h > lilBugPeak then
        begin
            lilBugPeak = high;
            lilBugPeakTime = t;
        end;
        if l < lilBugValley then
        begin
            lilBugValley = low;
            lilBugValleyTime = t;
        end;
        //can the worm transform to bull or bear bug
        if lilBugPeak - lilBugValley > bugDropRisePer * ATRValue then
        begin
            if lilBugValleyTime > lilBugPeakTime then
            begin
                lilBug = "bullBug";
//              print(d," ",t," ",lilBug," ",lilBugPeakTime," ",lilBugValleyTime);
            end;
        end;

        if lilBugPeak - lilBugValley > bugDropRisePer * ATRValue then
        begin
            if lilBugValleyTime < lilBugPeakTime then
                lilBug = "bearBug";
//          print(d," ",t," ",lilBug," ",lilBugPeakTime," ",lilBugValleyTime);
        end;

    case("bullBug"):
        if rsi(c,rsiLen) crosses above bugOverSold and l < lilBugValley then
        begin
            lilBug = "bullButterfly";
        end;

    case("bullButterfly"):
        if time < calcTime(bugEndTime,bugEndTimeOffSet) and
        rsi(c,rsiLen) > bugOverSold then
            buy numSharesCons shares next bar at highest(h,numTrigBars) stop;
        value97 = value97 + 1;
        if value97 >= butterflyLife then
        begin
            lilBug = "";
            value97 = 0;
        end;

    case("bearBug"):
        if rsi(c,rsiLen) crosses below bugOverBot  and h > lilBugPeak then
        begin
            lilBug = "bearButterfly";
        end;
    case("bearButterfly"):
```

```
    if time < calcTime(bugEndTime,bugEndTimeOffSet) and
    rsi(c,rsiLen) < bugOverBot then
        sellShort numSharesCons shares next bar at lowest(l,numTrigBars) stop;
    value96 = value96 + 1;
    if value96 >= butterflyLife then
    begin
        lilBug = "";
        value96 = 0;
    end;

end;
SetStopPosition;
setStopLoss(loss$);
setProfitTarget(profit$);


setExitOnClose;
```

$$\triangle\triangle\triangle$$

```
//Function PackDailyBars - will be explained in Advanced Topics
inputs: startTimeTrigger(numericSimple),endTimeTrigger(numericSimple),
periodsBack(numericSimple),
myOpen[w](numericArrayRef),
myHigh[x](numericArrayRef),
myLow[y](numericArrayRef),
myClose[z](numericArrayRef),
useSettlement(trueFalse),settlementTime(numericSimple),
settlementFormula(numericSimple);

vars:arrIndex(0),dayHi(0),dayLo(99999999),dayOp(0),dayCl(0),daySettle(0),
triggerA(False),triggerB(False);
vars: iCnt(0),jCnt(0),doShuffle(false);


triggerA = false;  //open bar
triggerB = false;  //close bar

//did we hit the startTimeTrigger exactly
triggerA = t = startTimeTrigger + barInterval;g
//or is it missing say 1805 is open time and
//t[1] = 1700 and t = 1810
if t[1] <= startTimeTrigger and t > startTimeTrigger + barInterval and
    triggerA = False then
        triggerA = True;
//if open then set dayOP to open
//       set dayHi to 0
//       set dayLo to nine 9s
if triggerA then
begin
    dayOp = o;
```

```
        myOpen[0] = dayOp;
        dayHi = 0;
        dayLo = 999999999;
        dayCl = 0;
end;

//collect daily highs and daily lows
if h > dayHi then dayHi = h;
if l < dayLo then dayLo = l;

//did we hit the endTimeTriger exactly
if t = endTimeTrigger then triggerB = True;
// or is it missing say 1700 is close time and
// t[1] 1655 and t = 1805
value1 = 0;
if t[1] < endTimeTrigger and t > endTimeTrigger then
begin
        value1 = 1;
        triggerB = True;
end;
// if close then set myHigh[0] and myLow
//if triggerB = False then
//begin
        myHigh[0] = dayHi;
        myLow[0] = dayLo;
        myClose[0] = c;
//end;
if t = settlementTime then
begin
        if settlementFormula = 1 then daySettle = close;
        if settlementFormula = 2 then daySettle = (h+l)/2;
        if settlementFormula = 3 then daySettle = (h+l+c)/3;

end;
if triggerB then
begin
        dayCl = c[value1];
//     print("shuffling from ",minList(periodsBack,arrIndex)," to 2");
        for iCnt = minList(periodsBack,arrIndex) downto 1
        begin
                myOpen[iCnt] = myOpen[iCnt-1];
                myHigh[iCnt] = myHigh[iCnt-1];
                myLow[iCnt] = myLow[iCnt-1];
                myClose[iCnt] = myClose[iCnt-1];
        end;
        myOpen[0]  = dayOp;
        myHigh[0]  = dayHi;
        myLow[0]   = dayLo;
        myClose[0] = dayCl;
        if useSettlement then myClose[0] = daySettle;
        arrIndex   = arrIndex + 1;
end;
if arrIndex < periodsBack then
        packDailyBars = -1
```

else
        packDailyBars = 1;

APPENDIX B-LINKS TO VIDEO INSTRUCTION

L inks to videos- Here are the links to the video instructions for each tutorial. Remember Tutorial 20 has two videos.

Tutorial 14: https://vimeo.com/629249948/6b07523716

Tutorial 15: https://vimeo.com/636590659/3bdd1b38d3

Tutorial 16: https://vimeo.com/641159384/f65e09a5e3

Tutorial 17: https://vimeo.com/643965726/c406bd7589

Tutorial 18: https://vimeo.com/647343005/8f44dcf7e3

Tutorial 19: https://vimeo.com/652907344/b9e2a51370

Tutorial 20 Watch Me First:

 https://vimeo.com/655371775/b9378b9cea

Tutorial 20:https://vimeo.com/655115350/d9151bf1ab

Tutorial 21: https://vimeo.com/659396251/fcbed00c8f

Tutorial 22: https://vimeo.com/659394166/509a300465

Made in United States
Orlando, FL
29 January 2022